POLITICS
A Study of
Control
Behavior

POLITICS

A Study of Control Behavior

Neil A. McDonald

RUTGERS UNIVERSITY PRESS

New Brunswick, New Jersey

Permission to quote has been granted by the following:
The University of Michigan Research Center for Group Dynamics, Institute for Social Research, for permission to quote from Dorwin Cartwright, ed., Studies in Social Power.

The University of Michigan Press for permission to quote from Kenneth E. Boulding, The Image *(Copyright © 1956 by The University of Michigan).*

John Wiley & Sons, Inc., for permission to quote from Floyd Allport, Theories of Perception and the Concept of Structure.

Lady Barbara Ward Jackson for permission to quote from "The Illusion of Power," which appeared in Atlantic Monthly *(December, 1952).*

To ENOLA and OTTO
and the memory of EDNA

Preface

It is probably never quite possible to discover the precise source of one's notion of how things are, or of the kinds of things that fascinate one person. I really cannot remember a time when I was not aware of, and somehow involved in, something called politics. I am sure there was a time when my father did not serve on an election board, but it was either before I was born or before I had any remembered experiences. About the same can be said for his serving on the local school board. Campaigns, elections, debates, arguments, meetings, and affairs local, national, and international seem always to have involved me.

I now realize all of a sudden that without really having intended it in just the way it has worked out I have been involved in politics all of my life to now, and since I have no intention of uninvolving myself I suppose that means what it seems to mean. All of this makes it rather natural that I have from time to time speculated on what I have been about.

This book is about politics and control, or politics as control. The foregoing may shed some light on the source and manifestations of my interest in politics, but not in control and the particular formulation that is being presented here. This came later and was first given formal expression in my doctoral dissertation, where I examined the operations of the Federal work and work relief program of the Depression as a control problem. I suspect that Chester I. Barnard and his *The Functions of the Executive* was very important to me, but then so was Lincoln Steffens' *Autobiography*. My tastes always having been more theoretical than activist, my practical involvement always ended up as something to theorize and speculate about. In trying to find some meaning in my experiences and studies I underwent various degrees of immersion in the classical theorists. How I have been marked by this immersion is sometimes quite visible in the pages that follow, but visible or not the influence has been great and one day I hope to be more explicit about this. It probably shows that I am most fascinated and stimulated by Rousseau.

Somewhere along the way I encountered a few less wellknown but very important influences. Things never quite looked the same to me after I read Guglielmo Ferrero's, *Principles of Power*, the reports on the famous experiments at the Hawthorne plant of Western Electric, Henry Jones Ford's *The Rise and Growth of American Politics*, Graham Wallas', *Human Nature in Politics*, and John R. Commons' *The Legal Foundations of Capitalism*. Among the more contemporary, even in a very small list, I must single out John Dewey, Reinhold Niebuhr, Talcott Parsons, and Walter Lippmann.

So much for the very general. Now to those who had a more direct hand in the actual formulation. Aside from the very great involvement of the people to whom the book is dedicated, my wife, Enola, and my parents, the persons who have been most helpful are my colleague James Rosenau and his wife, Norah. They have contributed in generous measure readings, discussions, criticisms, and, above all, encouragement. I suppose that in one way or another all of my students have helped more than any of us know. I particularly want to single out students who have been in a course in contemporary political theory that I taught for several years, students in a senior seminar that Mr. Rosenau and I have taught jointly for a long time, several generations of Eagleton Fellows in Politics whom Don Herzberg and I taught in a seminar for a number of years, the Eagleton Institute of Politics and its very efficient and dedicated secretarial staff who duplicated a couple of versions of the manuscript. I want to thank Paul Tillett of the Eagleton Institute for reading several chapters of an early version of the manuscript and making many helpful comments. My thanks also go to Harry Bredemeier of Douglass College, who upon reading the manuscript gave me great encouragement.

Needless to say, none of the foregoing persons can share in the faults and shortcomings of the book, but whatever virtues are found here they all had a hand in creating them.

Contents

POLITICS
A Study of
Control
Behavior

Introduction

Why do people pay taxes, fight in wars, pay homage to rulers, obey policemen, and curb strong impulses to avenge wrongs or to take what they desire? The frequency of such behavior and such restraint is high. It is tempting to assume that this behavior is easy to understand because it is common. However, frequency is not necessarily related to simplicity or obviousness. To say of anything that it is widespread does not account for its character or its universality, nor does a thing's universality shed light on its causes or consequences.

An identifiable phenomenon can be regarded in one of two ways: it can be regarded as natural and obvious, inconceivable otherwise. Or the same phenomenon can be regarded as complex, mysterious, and, both in its existence and character, not at all self-evident. For example, it is quite possible to observe taxpaying behavior and to regard the reasons for it as simple and obvious. Direct fear of being put in jail is an example of a simple reason. But without changing the observed phenomenon at all, the observer may regard the behavior as unusual and highly complex.

This shift is illustrated in various ways. The observer can be puzzled by people's refusing to pay taxes, or he can regard such nonpayment as readily and simply explainable, and view the payment of taxes as an astonishing fact, quite mysterious in its causes. Again, an observer who is impressed by the degree to which man is powerfully and dominantly motivated by basic animal-like impulses and appetites may be surprised to reflect that the behavior called taxpaying may be differently motivated from the acts of eating when hungry and ceasing to eat when full.

So, it can be argued that if appetite rules all, taxpaying is indeed a mystery and takes a lot of explaining. This becomes clearer upon considering one distinctive characteristic of taxpaying. In its most basic sense, the paying of a tax is the surrendering of a value, whether that value be money, material, or work. But it is not the surrendering of a value that distinguishes a tax. The carrying out of any exchange or trade also involves the surrendering of a value. But exchange, trade, or purchase suggests that for the surrendered value a value is received in return; a word such as "exchange" implies a close, direct, and testable relation between what is given and what is secured. It constitutes what is usually called a transaction. Thus, taxpaying can be regarded as an exchange relation, but in so far as language reflects actual understanding, it is a widespread practice to differentiate the two.

Some time ago Russell Baker in his Observer column in the *New York Times* (April 12, 1964) made one aspect of this difference clear in an entertaining fashion. In the essay he tells the story of Brown, an imaginary taxpayer who, having paid $927.18 in income taxes, wants to know what his money is being used for. He is not satisfied at all to be told that a certain part of each tax dollar goes for defense, and so on. Brown wants to know what *his* $927.18 is being used for, not just any $927.18. Baker speculates on what might happen if Brown were told that his money was used to print ten pages of the *Congressional Record* at $90 per page. If he were told this, Baker thinks he might start reading the *Record* to see what he gets for his money, and the consequences of this would be unpredictable. Baker develops his piece to point out that paying taxes involves Negroes' supporting racists and John Birchers' supporting membership in the United Nations. Brown finally comes to realize that if his money is divided among all the costs of government he is not contributing enough to cut any ice in Washington and so he can be pushed around and made to feel insignificant. The government is seen here as a kind of conspiracy to keep Brown feeling insignificant.

> But let Brown know the truth—that he is the man who buys Senator Dirksen's cigarettes, who helped pay for the President's dinner last night, or who owns a piece of a nuclear submarine somewhere in the Arctic—let Brown know this, and you make him a menace to government.

In this amusing piece Baker brings out an aspect of all taxes: the lack of a clear and direct relationship between what one pays in and what one receives in return. As compared with any ordinary purchase transaction, the value that the taxpayer surrenders is just as specific, direct, and understandable as the value surrendered in exchange for a car. But that which is received in return is different. The return for taxes paid is about as general, indirect, and remote as the car purchased is specific, tangible, near, and direct, for the car's capacity for gratification and utility is determinate.

The foregoing discussion has attempted to make some of the ideas that are widely believed to be true about the human

species consistent with the surrender of values involved in pur-
chases and trades, and to emphasize that if accepted as fully
explaining behavior taxpaying appears as highly unusual behavior, running counter to what we would expect if all interpersonal relations resembled transactions. This does not mean
that taxpaying is *really* unusual or *really* commonplace and
simple, but rather that there can be a basis for either emphasis.
The one we use will depend upon what puzzles or fascinates
us.

Paying homage to rulers, going to wars, obeying policemen,
and curbing strong impulses even when a person is certain
that he could act on the impulse with impunity—all of these
and many more can be treated in the same way. The characteristic that is exciting to contemplate is the difference between
the directness and obviousness of a sacrifice, and the vague-
ness, indirectness, or remoteness of the return.

The central concerns of this book are those behaviors which
tend to be widespread and regular and which require sacrifices,
outputs, and restraints, but in which there is no obvious return
or satisfaction. The paying of taxes, for example, can be
treated as a mystery in three senses. It is a mystery that people
give up good, tangible, and understandable values for such
vague and unspecified returns; it is especially strange that
they give up these values when they could probably get by
easily without doing so; and, finally, why does the whole
process of collecting and spending tax money take the form
that it does? Why, for example, is the tax revenue used for
about the same things in all parts of the world, and for about
the same things today as yesterday and long ago?

These problems are not new. In the opening lines of his
Social Contract, Rousseau posed these arresting questions:

> Man is born free; and everywhere he is in chains. One thinks
> himself the master of others, and still remains a greater slave

than they. How did this change come about? I do not know. What can make it legitimate? That question I think I can answer.

The task Rousseau set for himself in the *Social Contract* was to find the basis for moral obligation to the political order. In working out his explanation he sheds a great deal of light on the logical implications of a political order. Implicitly he has many things to say about what has to be true and what must happen to account for the very existence of the political or civil order. The form of Rousseau's inquiry, however, is moral. He asks, why *should* man obey, or under what conditions should he obey? The question that he does not ask directly is why *do* men obey, or under what conditions do men obey?

This book is a speculation on Rousseau's indirect question. It is the question of what must be true if we are to account for the existence of an ordering of human affairs in which, among other things, there is widespread taxpaying, going to war, paying homage to certain people, and specific restraints and deferences. A political order, an order with certain characteristics (to be stated shortly), is taken as the point of departure. Given that point, an attempt is made to state the conditions necessary and sufficient for its existence.

The procedure followed here is simple. It is to identify and describe certain behavior, and its patterns, then to suggest tentatively what must be true for such behavior patterns to exist and persist, and finally to work out some of the consequences. There is nothing revolutionary about the method used here, but an understanding of the inquiry requires that the method be understood.

The first step is to fix attention on behavior that can be observed and its pattern or regularity described in behavioral terms. This is to say that taxpaying is to be thought of in the first place as individuals handing over money or specific values to other persons, with the many handing to the few. An election regarded like this would not be thought of as a law or constitutional provision or elected officials, but rather as great aggregates of people who for a short, fixed period set aside their other activities and go to certain places, where they mark a piece of paper or pull the lever of a machine.

Having identified and described the pattern in behavior terms, the next step is to explain it. For example, given our existing level and kinds of knowledge of people, what do we think accounts for such behavioral regularity? What brings it into existence? More formally, what are the necessary and sufficient conditions for the existence of the particular pattern?

In formulating a tentative answer to this question there would be produced at some level what is commonly called "theory." In the sense in which the word "theory" is used here its distinctiveness is mainly a matter of form. Theory is an attempt, expressed in any language, to explain a phenomenon by means of logic and experience. The results of theorizing may be regarded as good, bad, or indifferent, useful or useless, simple or complex, broad-gauged or narrow-gauged, general or particular. It is theory if it *attempts* to explain or account for some behavior.

There is a whole category of patterned interaction that is puzzling. It is a category in which acts of compliance are not readily accounted for, either by the notion of relating means to ends to gratify appetites, or by the notion of automatic responses to stimuli, or by any simple and direct relation between end sought and means used.

It is intriguing that so many people pay taxes, and that a pattern is made by the time, place, amount of payment, and uses to which the money is put. If people give up some good or value in order to gratify their appetite for food, we say they are hungry and we know how to satisfy their appetite; but what can we say are the reasons they give up a particular amount of tax money for ends that are largely vague and in-determinate?

Contemplation of the strange behavior of paying taxes leads us to suggest that perhaps there is a category of behavior which is an outgrowth of concerns and needs not strictly analogous to appetites and the direct relating of means to ends. This behavior may result from concern about what is here called man's *more remote environment*. Possibly a man's concern with a world only dimly knowable because it is too large for him to experience directly might inspire him to make sacrifices and to behave in the interest of stabilizing and controlling it. How would man act, what patterns would develop, what problems would arise, if we posited him as being universally concerned with ordering the more remote environment? Is this type of concern similar in its universality to the concern for food, clothing, shelter, and companionship? Is it equally capable of leading to practices and patterns directly related to needs?

It seems plausible to argue that in such acts as paying taxes or paying homage man behaves as we might expect him to if he *needed* to pay taxes or *needed* to pay homage—otherwise such behavior would not be universal. But one cannot jump from the "need" to pay taxes to concern with the more remote environment unless the payment of taxes is related to controlling, regulating, or improving the taxpayer's more remote environment. This suggests a relation between awareness of, and concern about, a more remote environment and the control of that environment. The basic need, then, would be to control the more remote environment, with taxpaying understood as a vague and general means to that end. That class of acts and pattern of acts that seem to be most satisfactorily explained by the means and implications of controlling the more remote environment we call *politics*.

Thus, control is the master concept and process in accounting for a particular patterned interaction. There are three kinds of situation in which the notion of control is especially useful and interesting.

First, there are those cases of patterned interaction in which it is clear that unless deliberate or calculated steps were taken to create and sustain it, the pattern would not persist. We are especially interested in those patterns which seem to be induced by deliberate control acts. In other words, we are mainly interested in deliberate or calculated control acts and their uses, consequences, and limitations.

Second, as a pattern encompasses more people, more roles, more time or space—as any of these variables or any combination of them increases—the various aspects of deliberate control acts affecting the pattern become more fascinating. We shall call the more remote environment any kind of increase in temporal, spatial, and functional distance, or degree of remoteness. It is the remoteness component that distinguishes a tax payment from a transaction. It also explains why we find an election more interesting than the purchase of groceries.

Third, there is the widespread use of appeals made to people to conform their behavior in certain ways for the good or love of some entity or unit, such as "the system," "the state," or "the community." It will be argued later that as remoteness and deliberateness in control increase, the explicitness and frequency of appeals to the feelings for the unit or entity increase.

Hence, we are interested in those interaction patterns that encompass greater diversity; we are especially interested in the role that deliberateness or calculation plays; and we are more especially interested in the part played in control by the control *system*, perceived as a unit or entity.

There is an identifiable order in human affairs, for large aggregates of people behave with distinctive unity and uniformity; they engage in common undertakings and appear to consent to some kind of behavioral guidance which produces and reflects patterns of interpersonal relations. This apparent ordering in human affairs requires that people behave in certain ways to form one pattern rather than another, or, indeed, to form a pattern rather than a nonpattern. For example, one can observe patterned interaction and note the pattern, and then imagine behavioral changes that would alter or destroy it. Since there is no "natural" date for paying taxes, it is easy to think that paying on April 15 is required by something. Thus any orderliness may be thought of as the set of prescribed behaviors necessary to constitute the order.

Of all the things that individuals in a given aggregate are required to do to interrelate their behavior with others, a distinction may be made between behavior that is natural and autonomous, and that which we think of as induced or externally brought about. An individual will engage in the first without cues or guidance: we expect people to eat when they are hungry, or to make exchanges in order to get food. However, we do not expect the other category of behavior to fall into a particular and steady pattern unless there are extrinsic cues, inducements, or directions. It is quite easy to think of a category of patterned interrelated behavior which does not seem likely to occur, or to occur in the particular pattern, unless some actions were deliberately taken to bring it about—to ensure that it was one way and not another. Taxpaying is an example. We do not expect a given large aggregate of people to turn over a certain amount of money at a specific time and place. Thus, in accounting for large-scale uniform and unified behavior we are led to suggest that some control is being exercised.

If we are unable to account for large numbers of people paying taxes except by positing the existence of control acts which cause the payment, or are a necessary condition for the payment pattern, we are led to a distinction between a control act and process and a response act and process. At this point we may ask ourselves why so many people respond to control acts in a manner that creates unity and uniformity rather than nonunity and nonuniformity. In other words, why does an individual respond to cues and various control acts of others rather than following his own bent, and why does he respond in one particular way rather than in another?

The basic conjecture here is that man acts as if he lives in at least two different but related worlds. One he knows mainly through his own experience. Through trial and error and negative-feedback learning he is able to respond either without extrinsic cues or by checking the soundness of the cues and substituting his own judgment as suggested by experience. This is his proximate world or environment. However, this world shades off into another about which he gradually develops some degree of awareness but which he knows only dimly, through sampling and fragments of direct experience. In this world direct relation between cause and effect fades. This we shall call a world of greater or increasing remoteness.

In this conjecture all men are seen as having some awareness of a more remote world, but the degree and complexity of the remoteness perceived will vary widely between and within cultures. However, as a result of this awareness, certain anxieties and concerns may arise. By doing certain things which otherwise are hard to explain, such as paying taxes, man acts as if he wants this more remote environment neutralized, simplified, utilized to support his aspirations and needs. In short, he wants to reduce its alien character, to tame or order it so that it is not inimical to him and cannot derange his more immediate world. In response to requests and cues he acts to bring this about.

However, wanting this world controlled and reasonably orderly is one thing, and knowing how and being able to accomplish this are another. The simpler relation between ends and means and direct experience that an individual uses in his proximate environment does not stand him in such good stead here. Here he is called upon to act and to conform his behavior in situations where he cannot check the consequences of his acts. What should a person do when he feels impelled to act but does not quite know what to do? And if he reaches out for help and solidarity, whom does he follow? In this kind of situation we may not only ask why should he conform at all, but also why should he conform in one way rather than in another; and if he has to follow the cues of others why should he follow the cue of one person and not another?

When we consider the widespread existence of taxpaying, paying homage, obeying policemen, acting with restraint in the face of strong provocation to act otherwise, and a whole complex of behavior in which people seem to act mysteriously, we see that in many of these situations man acts as if he is aware of a wider environment. This wider environment may be seen as threatening or friendly, but not as neutral. Concern created by awareness, however, leads man to imagine this wider environment as finite and determinate. He behaves as if he were loyally attached to an environmental unit; he conforms his behavior to support and nourish this unit, which he thinks of as "his," which he shares with others whom he refers to as "we," and through which he relates to all others as "they." Man acts as if this response to the world is natural to him.

The purpose of this book is to discuss and develop some of the implications of this basic conjecture.

The order of presentation is as follows: in Chapter 1 the concept of control is developed, with special reference to the implications of exercising control over a more remote environment. This is followed by a chapter on the process by which control acts are forged into control schemes. Chapter 3 deals with the nature and role of the unit of control, here called a *polity*.

These rather basic chapters are followed by three, each of

which is based upon one method of control, with special adaptations for control of the more remote environment. But methods must be applied, and so three more chapters are concerned with those instruments of control which appear to be most universal in facilitating deliberate control over units of remote environment.

For the sake of simplicity, this part of the book is presented from the perspective of one who controls or performs deliberate control acts. But our more general concern is with a control system or scheme, and this involves not only the control acts but the responses. The effectiveness of any control act is determined in part by the resistance the respondents exhibit and also by such countercontrol acts as they undertake. Thus, in the last part of the book we consider in the light of the general scheme some of the more durable factors that shape responses to control acts.

ONE

The Elements of Politics

Control

This inquiry accepts without proof that under some conditions what one person does affects or modifies what another person might otherwise be expected to do. It further accepts the proposition that under some conditions there is a lawful relation between what one person does and what another person does; this is to say that under the same conditions what one person does will tend to affect another person in the same way. This makes possible a situation in which one person's behavior determines another person's. In such situations we say that there is a control relationship. This is a study of one aspect of control relationships, but before we can specify the nature of that one aspect, we must qualify some of the foregoing propositions.

In the first place, what one person does may affect what many other persons do and affect them uniformly or differentially; and conversely what many persons do may affect one person. In the second place, when we speak of one person determining the action of another, or one person's capacity for determining another's action, it is more useful and realistic to speak in the language of probability. Thus, we would say that it is highly probable that B did act F because A did act G, or that it is highly probable that A has the capacity to cause B to do act F. Throughout this inquiry we are dealing with relationships in which mechanical certainty, as distinguished from degrees of probability, has little use. In the third place, it is to be emphasized that nothing has been said so far that would limit the means, methods, techniques, and types of situations used to produce a control relationship. These are the factors that are to be examined.

In order to proceed with an inquiry into the control relationship, we must adopt an analytical distinction which it may not always be possible to establish empirically. This is the distinction between controller and respondent. In a control situation, as defined, we are always faced with related behavior, but the discrete acts performed are different, and they are the acts of separate individuals. Since the control relationship is one of differences, it is essential to have a convenient way of referring to each side of the relationship. Thus we distinguish between the control act and the response act. Analytically this distinction serves the same purpose as distinguishing between right and left, and just as we depend mostly on accepted conventions about which is right and which is left, so we shall rely mostly on conventions about which is control act and which is response act. Empirical inquiry may demonstrate that the difference in the relationship that has been postulated is reversed but our attention will have been drawn to the phenomenon and its components by the analytical distinction.

The common-sense difference between the control act and the response act is based mainly upon lapsed time. The act that is first in actual time or is first anticipated, tends to be regarded as the control act, and is followed in time by the response act. Along with time lapse, however, there develop common-sense notions about which is the cause act and which is the effect act. In attempting to trace the interplay of the two we learn a great deal about the nature of the control process. Some of these common-sense notions have to do with relative roles and statuses and the use of control instruments.

In its most general sense the concept of control has to do with orderliness or lawfulness in the relations between two or more different phenomena. By adopting the controller-responder distinction we imply a similarity between control and response on the one hand and cause and effect on the other. By definition we have limited ourselves here to interpersonal control, but the general concept is applicable wherever there appears to be pattern or orderliness in relations between different phenomena.

The first step in limiting the aspect of control with which we are concerned here, and at the same time in declaring our perspective, is to distinguish between the impulses that initiate the control act. Most human beings are capable of eliciting a response from some other person. This being the case, and assuming, as we have, some free will, we can distinguish between control acts deliberately and purposefully undertaken to affect the behavior of another person in a particular manner, and those determining acts which are performed for any reason that is not intentional. This distinction is not based on some difference in the character of the acts themselves, or even on their consequences, but rather on that which prompts the undertaking. It will be argued subsequently that, except for the most elementary control situations, acts undertaken for control purposes tend to be distinctive. But for the present we want only to declare the distinction between intentional and unintentional control acts and to suggest that there are commonly accepted indicators to help us identify these differences. For example, the controller may indicate his intentions by verbal or other symbolic expressions. Thus if one man asks another to do something we assume that he asked him for the express purpose of getting him to do it. It might be shown empirically that the asker intended some other result, or a psychoanalyst might show the unconscious purpose in his request, but the control act would still take the *form* of a deliberate control act.

Thus, we shall call those control acts which are undertaken to evoke a particular behavior calculated, intentional, deliberate, or conscious, regardless of their success or failure or the indirectness and complexity between them and response acts —and at the moment we shall not make any particular distinction between the four adjectives. This limitation on our concern with control means that the unintended effects of acts are relevant only as they affect the deliberate control relationship.

The second limitation to be imposed and perspective to be declared has to do with a factor that we shall call remoteness. As the quality of remoteness in a control relationship increases, so does our interest in that control relationship. This is but another way of saying that we are primarily interested in control under the conditions of increasing remoteness.

What is this quality of remoteness? In its most general sense remoteness implies indirectness and lack of obviousness in the relations between two or more objects or acts. Usually remoteness increases as space, time, or sparsity of preexisting relations increases. As deliberate control is exercised over, or in the face of, increasing remoteness, it partakes more of the political as the term is used here. The basic relationships affected by variations in remoteness are those between controller and respondent, between controller and the hierarchy of ends in view that guide his control acts, and between respondent and the ends in view that condition the response. There are, in turn, three kinds of remoteness, any one of which, any combination of which, or all of which may affect control. These we shall call spatial, temporal, and functional.

Increasing space between any of the relationships involved in a control situation may or may not appreciably decrease the directness and obviousness of control acts; it is not likely to increase them.

The second kind of distance is time. The lapse of time between the control act and the response act may be small or great. Another aspect of the time factor is what might be called endurance. A control act or a set of control acts may be thought of as maintaining effective control over a long or a short period of time. The greater the time distance and endurance, the greater the interest. We shall study the time factor by trying to understand the conditions under which control is exercised over longer time spans.

What we have called functional remoteness has to do with increasing complexity and lack of obviousness that may arise because of the degree of familiarity and preexisting relatedness at the time the control process is undertaken. For any controller, getting a stranger to do something presents a special type of problem, and a controller whose end in view is unfamiliar will have different problems and will possibly need different methods than one who is seeking a well-established and thoroughly familiar goal.

As any one of the three kinds of distance increases between control act and response act and between control or response act and end in view, we become more interested in exploring the implications. The most intriguing kind of control relationship would thus be one in which all three kinds of distance or remoteness applied to all three basic relationships: for example, a situation whereby a controller in the present time establishes control over unborn persons, who when born will live on the moon, their prior relationship no more than the sharing of a common universe, all for the end in view of insuring justice on some third planet. What is suggested here is that there would be a limit to what one could learn about such a process by studying parental control of children.

One of the major contentions of this inquiry is that as distance and deliberateness in control increase between control act and response act and between control and response act and end in view, a distinctive control system emerges as a unit or entity, and that the widespread perception of this entity as an object comes to play an increasingly important role in effecting the control. This entity is described as a perceived unit of the more remote environment. The reasons for specifying the "perceived" aspect will be developed later. For the moment we note that this unit will be called a polity.

This brings us to a discussion of why the activities, processes, institutions, perceptions, and beliefs which are most characteristically involved in extending deliberate control through distance or remoteness are here called political. In other words, the distinctiveness of that which is usually called political or politics is its involvement with deliberate control over intervening remoteness. It is to be further argued that the use of the word "political" to denote such activities arises from the central position of a polity in such control. Aristotle's *Politics* has to do with the affairs of a polity and it may also be regarded as dealing with the phenomenon of deliberate control over remoteness. The same may be said of Plato's *The Republic* and most of the other classics of politics.

The remainder of this inquiry will be devoted to exploring the limited kind of control relationship that has been described and roughly distinguished. But before turning to that task, it will be helpful in clarifying the control concept to show how it relates to the works of other writers and to suggest reasons why what we call politics has a universality deeply rooted in human nature.

Control has not been generally recognized as the central active element of politics to the degree that the facts seem to warrant. Political speculation has always dealt with control, for what is commonly called politics has to do with some men trying to get others to act in certain ways. Let us look at some of the reasons that the word "control" has been avoided.

In modern times the rise of democracy as a fact and as a value tends to emphasize self-control, and on the verbal level self-government tends to be substituted for self-control. Although political activity is regarded as desirable, there is a natural tendency to deny the characteristic control aspect, because deliberate control of some by others is regarded as contrary to the idea of democracy. In Utopian democracy, each person controls himself and, in turn, the government, by uniform autonomously willed action. Thus all kinds of circumlocutions are used to create the illusion that the essential process of control can be retained without fully recognizing its implications.

A closely related explanation for the tendency to avoid the notion of politics as deliberate control of people by people, and one that better accounts for the reluctance to face control candidly in predemocratic times, is the universal tendency for man to glorify man. Speculation about the nature of man has always been the province of priests and philosophers. The philosopher tends to distinguish man from brute and to emphasize the rational and self-directing nature of man. The priest is also concerned with man, but with man as the gods' special object of attention, emphasizing the gods' control of man, not one man's control over another. But the development of knowledge should release us from such black-and-white viewpoints. Man today easily acknowledges that much of his life is determined by natural nonhuman events, and he should thus be able to realize that invariably some of his actions are determined by deliberate acts of persons he does not know, often against his will. If this were not so, social life would be impossible.

We can suggest one more explanation for the reluctance to

acknowledge the central importance of deliberate control in politics (which will be developed more fully at a later point). An important technique by which some persons control other persons, especially strangers, is to disguise the control acts by attributing them to impersonal and nonhuman sources. Plato described this process with unmatched clarity in his myth about the fundamental difference between the persons made of gold and those made of baser metals. A political system is always strengthened by attributing control acts performed under it to something other than mere frail human will.

A consideration of why the element of deliberate control seems to have been understated and circumvented in much of the speculative material on politics leads rather naturally to a discussion of power, which, it is to be argued here, has been a kind of halfway house on the road to the acknowledgment of the basic nature of deliberate control. Generally speaking, those who have tried to establish the distinctive nature of "the political" have taken the position that either the "state" or "power" is the key element. The state is, however, merely a highly formalistic and perhaps transitory kind of polity, or great society or unit, which is an outgrowth of control efforts and only indirectly and instrumentally the cause of them. In recent years there has been a tendency for the more realistic, more scientific, and less formalistic political inquirers to develop the notion that what they call power is the basic stuff of politics. What is the essential difference between power and control as we have defined the latter concept? Why did power appear so attractive to those who began to apply systematic methods of inquiry to political behavior? Let us take up the question of difference first.

One of the more obvious differences between control and power is that "control" is essentially a verb and "power" is essentially a noun. This point is as important as it is obvious. Yet it has not been explored. Robert Dahl, in an article entitled

"The Concept of Power,"[1] notes but does not develop this characteristic of the word "power." Although a serviceable noun can be made out of control, an equally serviceable verb cannot be made from power. To empower something is to give it power, but the act in this case is that of giving. Likewise, to power something suggests rather awkwardly to supply energy, but it does not express any sense of direction or purpose for the energy, or anything about the nature of the energy.

Now this excursion into semantics might seem overly pedantic. But is it? To deal fundamentally with behavior and action one must use verbs and nouns appropriately. Power is always an inference and cannot even in theory be directly observed. Therefore, unless its observable components can be specified and described, it has little scientific or theoretical usefulness. Even the phrase "power relation," commonly used in discussing politics, is a static rather than a dynamic concept, and if power refers to a quality it must designate specific qualities. Control, even in its noun form, implies correlative action, and in its verb form it suggests a class of related specific acts. Power, however, suggests a very general natural phenomenon and attributes false concreteness to it. It suggests something that can be touched, packaged, and measured. It implies a phenomenon that has been stopped for a split second, rather than a reciprocating continuum or process. Thus, it is not hard to understand why the concept of power has been of so little value in directing research and why decision-making has provided a far more fruitful concept for empirical inquiry.

Further facts should be noted. Most definitions of the noun "power" imply that it is a capacity or ability to do something. Both the root and the formal definitions emphasize ability; but instead of regarding power as that aspect of an action which predicts ability to order interaction in a certain way, there has been a tendency to use power as an ingredient or substance in an interaction pattern or in a relationship. Thus we have phrases like "who has the power," "A has power over B," "power need not be bad."

In theoretical development of social phenomena, power as a concept is somewhat analogous to phlogiston in the development of physical theory. It will be remembered that Stahl in 1702 advanced a theory of fire which postulated "phlogiston," as a material substance which was disengaged in the process of combustion and which in some way was responsible for fire. There was even a verb form, "phlogisticate," meaning "to combine with phlogiston."

It was noted earlier that there was a good explanation for the concentration on the power concept when scholars first began to break away from excessive formalism and legalism. Conceptualizing as a "something" called power the capacity of a person to exact exceptional response and deference is natural as a stage or a halfway house. It is no longer enough, as empirical and theoretical works in the social sciences are beginning to demonstrate.

A few further observations are in order. Politics in study and practice has always been and will always be concerned with rulers, officials, and laws. But in the older approach the ruler's effectiveness was attributed to some object that conferred an extraordinary capacity and right to control the more remote environment—the mystic quality of majesty, the law, the crown, the mace, the scepter, or the ceremonies. As it was observed that people without crown, law, and scepter often evoked the same kind of response as those who possessed them, these symbols came to be regarded as the effects, rather than the causes, of power. However, a ruler's power was still thought to lie in some tangible object not possessed by others. Those with extraordinary capacity to evoke responses from strangers were said to have political power, but they were still regarded as *having* something and their behavior was examined in this light. Patterns of interpersonal behavior, not possessions, must be the perspective for the study of politics, and modified symbols for orderly discourses must reflect this change.[2]

Another aspect of the power concept has to do with drawing analogies between property, money, and politics. It was recognized early in our history that property was useful in controlling other people. Those who owned property were able to exercise a special influence or control over others. As money came to play a more important role in human affairs, it was observed that people who had money were able to exercise even more control over others; money was thought to have a mystical quality which conferred something on its possessor. Then, when it was observed that some people were able to affect the behavior of many people, including strangers, it was asumed that the source of their control was similar to property or money. Thus, they were said to have power, either military power, or a more general version, which came to be called political power. Money does have a physical existence, and variations in its physical qualities are related to variations in responses to it. If money is regarded as conferring a general but not unlimited capacity for achieving desired ends, then money is power. The same is true of property. But the nature of both money and property is only revealed through the behavior they evoke, and they only evoke selective behavior that is somewhat predictable but culturally and politically limited. Both money and property are effective instruments to control the more remote environment and are therefore laden with political content. We are mainly concerned, however, with what people have, whether it be money, power, or property, so that we can predict what they will do and what they will cause others to do.

The shift from an exclusive preoccupation with such formal and static concepts as sovereignty, law, and state to a concern with what people have was indeed a step forward in the development of political theory. However, we must now have a concept of acts, not of possessions or things. What is suggested here is a concept of control, and, for the more limited purposes of politics, deliberate control of events and acts in the more remote environment.

There are marked differences between the operation of deliberate control in the more remote environment and in the more intimate environment. John Dewey, in his *The Public and Its Problems*,[3] distinguished between the direct and indirect consequences of acts. He also insisted that the social consequences of acts are modified and shaped by both natural and non-natural barriers, which tend to prevent and limit the spread of consequences. He argued that the behavioral boundaries of an extensive association tend to be coterminous with such barriers. Dewey did not sufficiently distinguish between the perception of the consequential acts and the perception of the unit, but he did in effect differentiate between the remote and the close-at-hand world and the personal and impersonal world, emphasizing that the latter is not a mere extension of the former. These distinctions call attention to the difference between attempting to induce desired behavior in people who are far away in functional, spatial, and temporal terms, and those who are more proximate.

Throughout this discussion of control a distinction has been drawn between control in general and that which is calculated or deliberate. At first glance the adjectives "calculated" and "deliberate" might seem unnecessary, since the very phrase "human control" implies intentional or purposive action; but because the word "control" is often used in three contexts, it is advisable to use the modifier. First, there is control attributed to a supernatural will, which often takes the form of postulating an anthropomorphic god who engages in deliberate control action over men. Although the term "human" has not been used along with deliberate control, it should be perfectly clear that the control acts under scrutiny here are those of the human species and not those of beasts or gods. Second, there is a tendency to regard any action pattern, with its characteristics of regularity, systematicness, and predictability, as being a product of control. The ostensibly random, unpatterned, or capricious act is said to be uncontrolled and all others are controlled, although the source of control is unspecified.

Finally, there is the situation in which a person's act elicits a certain response that suggests to the outside observer a causal relationship, but in which the actor did not intend to produce this correlative effect.[4] The modifiers "calculated" or "deliberate" are used especially to distinguish between intended and unintended consequences. Adam Smith argued in *Wealth of Nations* that a nation will maximize its wealth if the government does not interfere in the economy. He voiced a profound truth when he called attention to the fact that persons pursuing one end may, individually or collectively, produce better-patterned and more highly desirable consequences than they can by deliberate pursuit of objectives. Perhaps a wealthy nation and a beautiful and harmonious economic order never came about by each person tending to his own business and maximizing his own profits as Smith's followers argued, but the classical economists accurately distinguished between the deliberate and the unintentional, and they further saw that the political order was primarily concerned with the deliberate and the general rather than the unintentional and the specific. On this basis they argued for limits to political action, contending that a better, more rational remote environment would come about automatically than would come about by design and intention via the political.

Seemingly self-generated patterns of interaction do appear in human affairs and upon being perceived they not only form still further patterns but may also serve as institutions of control by their mere existence, their perception, and by being affected or by some process of generating feeling. Nor can there be any doubt that these patterns and their perception are very much the concern of the student of politics. But the political scientist studies them from the peculiar perspective of achieving deliberate control. About the first thing the deliberate controller encounters is the existing patterns people have just perceived or formed as a stable image. Part of a controller's concern is the relationship between intended and unintended acts, and the consquences of the relationship.

In discussing control it is easy to give the impression that man is always trying to alter his environment, but much of what he does with reference to the world, both in its close-at-hand and more remote dimensions, is to adjust to it in terms of his perception and experience. The concept of control still applies, however, and it would be pointless to attempt an ultimate distinction between controlling and adjusting, for life is a reciprocal process. The difference between the deliberate and the unintended still stands: in part we adjust to the environment automatically and apparently without conscious thought. However, we also not only have a choice about what adjustment we will make, but about the choices of others who try to have us adjust in one way rather than another.

Barbara Ward, a well-known commentator on political and economic affairs, took up the matter of control some years ago, in an article entitled "The Illusion of Power." [5] Commenting on the rise and decline of the notion that man can in some measure control his own destiny and fashion the world in which he lives, she points out the similarity between the belief in automatic and unwilled progress and a rather fatalistic assumption of human irrationality, ushered in by the new scientific outlook. She notes that from this background there has emerged in more recent times the belief that the methods of science can be applied to the deliberate control of human beings. Both the totalitarian and the humane efforts in the use

of science are manifestations of the changed outlook. She puts
the change this way:

> After a century of interest in conditioning and environment—
> an interest that has added permanent insights to our knowl-
> edge of human behavior—the pendulum is swinging back to
> the human being upon whom the external influences go to
> work. He is profoundly affected by his society—but in turn it
> bears his mark, and the more men strive to overcome the an-
> onymity and irresponsibility of mass civilization the more
> urgently they have to consider the quality of the individual
> citizen in it. As the *New Fabian Essays* suggest: "Every eco-
> nomic system, whether capitalist or socialist, degenerates into
> a system of privilege and exploitation unless it is policed by a
> social morality which can only reside in a minority of citizens."
> Or, as a considerably shrewder observer of human nature once
> put it, "The fault, dear Brutus, is not in our stars, but in our-
> selves"—not in our environment, our conditioning, our collec-
> tive excuses for individual irresponsibility, but in the choice of
> our moral will.

Miss Ward then goes on to argue that as the crucial importance of the human will in human affairs is again recognized it becomes necessary to find how men can be persuaded
to accept what she calls social responsibility.

According to Miss Ward's article, this book could be regarded as an argument for a realistic view of what man can
and does cause his fellow man to do. It is only by understanding how other individuals control us deliberately and how we
control them that we can understand an important aspect of
the social process. Both the pure and applied sciences are well
served by dispensing with such notions as, for example, that
of the state controlling us. There is no doubt that all kinds of
impersonal forces control us, but this inquiry is based on the
assumption that we are also controlled by the intentional acts

of other persons and that this aspect of control provides a useful perspective for studying human behavior and is therefore worthy of inquiry.

A few years ago at Yale University, Robert A. Dahl, a political scientist, and Charles E. Lindblom, an economist, undertook to isolate and study the common elements in economics and politics.[6] They developed two concepts, which they call rational calculation and control, and which they regard as two basic kinds of social processes. The term "power" is scarcely mentioned in the book. They assign a central importance to control, but the independent position assigned rational calculation is not entirely clear. Perhaps it can be explained by the fact that their perspective was somewhat shaped by their purpose of accounting for the common bond between economics and politics.

In the present discussion there is no distinction made between the rational and the calculated; in fact, the term "rational" has purposely not been used in order to avoid arguments about the meaning of rationality, with its implications of a detached and somewhat godlike observer. Instead, the distinction is made between calculated and noncalculated control. Dahl and Lindblom seem to have been prompted to make the distinction between calculation and control by their desire to bring unintended and unconscious control within the general rubric of control. The perspectives of economics require the discovery of bigger patterns among discrete acts, each of which is sharply limited in its more general control consequences. These investigators strongly believe that activities are not necessarily capricious because they are not deliberately and consciously controlled, an important point. Nevertheless, it seems that here the study of politics and economics fundamentally diverge. In the view taken in our inquiry, the perspective of politics is that of calculated control over the more remote environment; whereas the perspective of economics is more a study of the consequences of control action in the proximate world. That Dahl and Lindblom attach a central importance to the control concept is attested by the fact that the heart of the book is a consideration of control and controllers, or leaders and nonleaders, as they call them. Although the concept of rational calculation provides some of the perspective for examining control in general, the control concept dominates the study.

It is postulated here that politics is a matter of purpose and control. This brings us to the question of why people want to control the behavior of other people, and why people respond to control. We can suggest four particularly relevant reasons for a person's wanting to control other persons.

In the first place, he wants to reduce randomness and chance in the events and human acts that impinge upon him and make up a part of his perceived environment; that is, he wants to impose some degree of regularity and predictability.

Second, he wants to avoid necessity. This is, of course, paradoxical—that which is necessary is, by definition, unavoidable —but human history can be written in terms of man trying to escape doing what appears to be necessary. The psychological factor here is important. Some events, rather than being too random, are regarded as too certain; efforts to change or to adjust to change or to adjust to the certainty are related to the concept of control.

Third, there is the notion of controlling in order to accomplish specified objectives. Often when a person wants to achieve a goal, he must demand that other persons modify their behavior. The control he exercises over others is the means by which he achieves his objective—it is a by-product of his purpose.

Finally, there is a fourth objective of control, one whose existence is more debatable. All people probably get some psychological satisfaction out of merely exercising control over others. The doctrine of original sin, which deals with man's propensity to play God, contributes a profound insight in this area, as does Lord Acton's aphorism, "power tends to corrupt; absolute power corrupts absolutely."

Thus we contend that the universality of politics arises out of man's universal will to order his environment and to pursue a variety of goals which he sees as affected by his more remote environment.

In the control problem developed here, politics is given its distinctive form by the interplay of two basic elements. These we call *the good life* and *polity*. We turn now to a development of these elements.

The Good Life

Intentional or deliberate control grows mainly out of man's desire to make the elements in his environment more orderly and predictable. It is argued here that some of the observable regularity and predictability can be accounted for by the intervention of acts willed and performed by human beings. But many sets or patterns of acts can be made regular and predictable. When there is regularity, discrete acts are ordered; when there is control, acts are both ordered and directed. Jews were murdered in Germany under Hitler through the exercise and imposition of control. The liquidation of the Kulaks in the Soviet Union was a manifestation of deliberate control.

Though man has little choice but to desire the ordering of his environment, he may shape its direction or its ends. It is in light of this that we are led to a concern with preferences and values. Such notions help us account for the regularity we can observe and to explain different and changing control systems. Even those who study inorganic matter, or nonhuman life, must be concerned with the intrinsic character of their objects of inquiry; external forces alone will not account for what happens.

In the context of politics, the observations that have to be explained are those which reveal great aggregates of people expressing and acting out not only preferences in the face of choice but also *commonly* expressed and *commonly* acted-out preferences in the face of choice. The logically possible choices in any given situation approach infinity. There are fewer though still many empirically probable choices, and yet out of the possible choices there has to be a remarkable convergence of actually acted-upon preferences in order to bring about regularity and unity of pattern in an interaction. War furnishes us with the most dramatic example of convergence of behavior because it requires acts which override strongly held preferences. In other words, the kind of convergence of behavior that war entails requires that many human beings forego alternative action. This kind of behavior especially needs explanation.

The necessity for the student of politics to treat human values as political data creates special opportunities and special problems. The investigator shares with his subject matter a common humanity: he must be careful that "fellow-feeling" does not distort his observations. The student of politics assumes that some of his subjects' behavior is freely determined and hence is a result of choice. To conceive of these subjects as having choice without developing notions about what the choice should be in a given situation requires a strong will and a respect for detached study of cause-and-effect relations. Therefore, the student of politics must have a clear, disciplined, and professional mind.

It is common to speak of the basis of man's preferences as his values. John Dewey says in speaking of morals: "The foremost conclusion is that morals has to do with all activities into which alternative possibilities enter. For wherever they enter a difference between better and worse arises." [1] Following this observation we may define a value as a relatively stable notion of what is better and what is worse. When we assume that an alternative choice is available, we also assume that man has some basis for choosing alternative A over alternative B, and we use the word "value" to denote this basis. If there is a pattern in the choices that a person makes it is assumed that something imposes the pattern; we call this a value. A value is not the same as a choice; it underlies the choice and guides the choice. Where there is no choice we speak of necessity.

In identifying values it is useful to distinguish between two kinds of behavior patterns—verbal or symbolic, and nonverbal or nonsymbolic—and to understand the properties of each. An example of a verbal or symbolic behavior pattern is "Honesty is the best policy." The same idea could be expressed by "I prefer the company of honest men," or "When I have a choice I prefer honest action." From these symbolic representations we can conclude that the speaker holds honesty as one of his values and that the holding of this value imposes a regularity upon other statements he might make. We might also assume, although we cannot be completely sure, that, having verbally expressed this value as a guide to his behavior, when he actually makes a choice the value will be reflected in the nonverbal action he takes.

Another way of identifying values is by observing ethical behavior and inferring the nature of the underlying values. Thus, if a person always chooses to be honest we tend to assume that a certain value dictates his choice, regardless of his verbal expression of preferences. That a person's actions sometimes do not support his professed value is indicated by the value-laden word "hypocrite."

The student of causal political theory is interested in values mainly for causative and predictive purposes, and as such he is not more concerned with verbal expressions of values than with values inferred from nonverbal behavior. If at times he seems to be more occupied with verbal expressions it is only because of their special use in deliberate control of behavior.

Although the study of the ultimate nature of values is mainly the business of philosophers and theologians, values do play an important role in political theory and the theorist has a duty to understand the phenomenon as completely as possible. The philosophical school of logical positivism makes a sharp distinction between value and fact, and argues that a value can never be derived from a fact. A value, they say, is a demand, or a desire, and all that can be said about it is that it exists. To show that it is good or true one must appeal to still other values, until one finally ends up by saying that something is good simply because it is good. And logically one can persist if he recognizes that factual and value statements are two entirely different order of statements. Logical positivism leads clearly to the notion that values are mainly manifestations of feelings or emotions. They exist, they can be studied, they are important, but the superiority of one value over another can only be established within a scheme of posited values, and not by the use of factual evidence.

As a tool of analysis the contentions of the logical positivists have been useful in guiding inquiry. However, whether they correctly reflect the ultimate nature of the universe is open to question. It is quite possible for the mind to impose a wall between facts and values, but the empirical usefulness of this exercise is limited. One may argue, for example, that there is no perception of a fact without some evaluation; that rather than there being two worlds, of fact and of value, there are simply two perspectives from which all sense impressions must be viewed. One perspective alone reveals only a flat undifferentiated surface which makes no meaningful impression on the viewer.

One example will give some indication of the value of the logical positivists' contribution to political analysis. A standard political argument is that if something exists it is good; vested interests should not be disturbed. Under this principle, it is enough to show what interests in fact exist, to furnish an ethical argument against change. Thus a value is derived from a fact. The logical positivists have made the important point that the mere existence of anything does not prove or disprove its value unless the continued existence can in turn be referred to some end or purpose beyond mere existence.

Enough has been said to give some idea of the nature of moral values and the issues involved in establishing their ultimate nature. More along this line must be left to the philosophers; we must return to a discussion of another type of value. Moral or ethical values express judgments in terms of right and wrong or good and evil, and for the most part these moral judgments are applied to human acts. There is, however, another type of value or judgment, which we call aesthetic. Its evaluations are expressed in terms of beauty and ugliness, and are usually applied to objects or states of being. We may like or dislike some act or object and be attracted favorably or unfavorably to it, not because we regard it as morally good, but because we find it beautiful to contemplate. Without entering into a philosophical discussion, it is enough here that we call attention to the essential nature of aesthetic evaluation and suggest that we cannot account for choice-making behavior adequately unless we introduce the relevance of aesthetic considerations in political action. For example, it may be that loyalty to a polity is in many instances more adequately explained by the notion of attraction to beauty than by notions of good and evil. It is difficult to read Plato or Edmund Burke, once this distinction has been suggested, without noticing the predominance of aesthetic values over moral values. But more of this later.

The active element in politics is deliberate control. Thus the political scientist and practitioner is interested in deliberated control acts and deliberated and nondeliberated response acts and the reciprocity among them. We have tried to show that both moral and aesthetic values are of concern to the student of politics for two reasons. In the first place, to know what will be preferred when there is choice enhances the predictive aspects of politics. Second, a knowledge of the nature of values and of specific moral and aesthetic values held by a people of a culture can serve as a basis for control purposes. What people will do and what they can be induced to do when they have choice are matters of great importance for the student of politics.

Values must be dealt with in causal political theory because they are believed to be, or to shed light on, causal agencies. But before we can develop the role of values in a political theory, we must deal with value patterns or complexes.

Individuals have many different values, and each value may be thought of as a pattern. That is to say that, given the opportunity of choice, an individual will make the same choice in similar situations. If in several situations he chooses honesty over dishonesty, we say that honesty is one of his ethical values. If in other instances he consistently chooses one practice over others simply because he finds it more satisfying, we can say he chooses on the basis of his aesthetic values. However, when the individual finds the value-dictated choices incompatible, he is faced with a conflict. His values tell him not to steal, but they also tell him to care for his family. By stealing he can serve the latter value and care for his family. By not feeding his family he can serve the value that prohibits stealing, but he will destroy the value that enjoins him to care for his family. Moral values may conflict, or moral and aesthetic values may clash. To which value does he give preference, and on what grounds does he choose between conflicting values? The observation of behavior tells us that he does order his values when they come into conflict, and that there seems to be a pattern that grows out of the relating of values—in other words, a value that evaluates values. We are going to call the pattern that reflects an individual's ordering of his values, his conception of the good life.

The approach suggested here may be clarified by an analogy. There is a difference between *the* law and *a* law, the former being a system composed of many laws and rules and their relation to one another. Generally speaking, it is necessary to understand *the* law in order to understand *a* law in any depth. Where individual rules demand conflicting actions, *the* law helps to order the relations between the two rules. This suggests that we cannot really know the law by simply knowing all of the rules. The law is more than the sum of its parts; it is the principle which informs the rules. If we do not understand the scheme which orders the rules, we cannot predict the course of behavior imposed by a rule in various situations. Similarly, we do not understand a person's conception of the good life by merely understanding the specific values that guide his behavior. The analogy with law is not farfetched, for each law or rule may be viewed as reflecting a value, whereas *the* law suggests a widely shared concept of the good life.

The notion of the good life suggests the existence of a tendency more stable and perhaps more basic than any one value. The good life is a more comprehensive pattern or sorting device than a value. We know of a value, however, by the same means we know of the good life, through both verbal expression and inferences from behavior.

What we have called the good life is obviously related to what is often called ideology. In a book devoted to nineteenth-century thinkers, entitled *The Age of Ideology*,[2] the editor,

Henry D. Aiken, describes the change in philosophical thought ushered in by Kant, Fichte, Hegel, Marx, and others. Briefly, this was a change from a metaphysics that tried by understanding nature to serve science, to a metaphysics the function of which was to help man order nature subjectively. "Metaphysics," Aiken says, "was regarded by Descartes, and before him by Aristotle, as continuous with the inquiries of the social sciences, differing from them only in scope and primacy. For Fichte, on the contrary, its concern and its method essentially are practical, not theoretical; what it yields is not descriptions of matters of fact, but 'posits' or commitments that are essential to the conduct of life." [3] Speaking of writers like Herbert Spencer who believed they were scientific, Aiken comments: "Yet even with them one discerns that their philosophical interest is not in the facts as such but in the basic attitudes to which the facts, as they describe them, lend support." [4]

In ideology the conception of the nature of things is used indirectly and often unconsciously to prove the validity of a particular notion of the good life. The notion of the good life may be inferred from the ideology, but is not directly expressed. The conceptualization to which we give the name ideology thus suggests an important truth. What is regarded as the good life by any individual will depend in large measure upon his cognition of the nature of things as well as upon his preference. Or to put it another way, his preferences will be modified by his cognition. It follows then that preferences can be changed by changing understanding, and indeed we may say that ideologies are used to change preferences in a determinate manner by changing understandings. Ideological persuasion may work where ethical or aesthetic persuasion fails. But ultimately the content of an ideology, insofar as it is an ideology as distinguished from metaphysics or science, is determined by the end in view; and thus the conception of the good life as used here is regarded as a more basic category and tool of analysis. One might say that in order to discover notions of the good life one must consider direct verbal expressions in the form of descriptions of ideally desired states, make inferences from ideologies, and make inferences from behavior in choosing between values.

Descriptions of any good life are rare. Eastern philosophies tend to deal more directly with the actual good life and emphasize the aesthetic component; whereas in the West, with its greater theoretical emphasis, we find more discussions of what kind of thing a conception of the good life is, and what are its necessary components. In the West we look more to our poets and artists for descriptions, and even these are few. One can find in Walt Whitman a celebration and description of the good life. Dante in *Paradiso* describes the good life rather than pondering its nature, and for a modern philosopher, Jacques Maritain, in *The Person and Common Good*, comes close to describing a good life. But for the most part our verbal expressions concerning the good life are in terms of principles or requisite conditions. George Santayana stresses an aesthetic principle as a basis for ordering preferences:

My own sympathies go out to harmony in strength, no matter how short-lived. The triumph of life lies in achieving perfection of form; and the richer and more complex the organism is that attains this perfection, the more glorious its perfection will be and the more unstable. Longevity is a vulgar good, and vain after all when compared with eternity. It is the privilege of the dust and the lowest and most primitive organisms. The gods love and keep in their memories the rare beauties that die young. I prefer the rose to the dandelion; I prefer the lion to the vermin in the lion's skin. In order to obtain anything lovely, I would gladly extirpate all the crawling ugliness in the world.[5]

We must conclude that the study of verbal expressions yields little about the preference that arranges and integrates values. This being the case we must observe, study, and make inferences from behavior, a process which leads to a rather startling conclusion: whatever else it is or is not, the good life is a polity or political life. It is amazing how many values people will subordinate in order to preserve their polity. Contemporary constitutional democrats have made only marginal modifications of the old doctrine of *raison d'état*. Individuals who thoroughly believe that human life is to be preserved set aside this value quite readily when it conflicts with defense of the polity. People give up their lives to preserve the polity, and they are widely praised for doing so. It has often been observed that the same kind of moral code does not apply in dealings between representatives of different polities, but all this usually means is that when the polity is involved, other values are subordinated.

Freedom is often said to be a supervalue in the West, and democracy a well-nigh universal supervalue nowadays. Yet in all cultures freedom is permitted and supported as a determining value only to the point where it is not viewed as destructive to polity value or to polity life. Treason is universally the most serious crime an individual can commit, which can only be explained by assuming that the maintenance of the polity is an ultimate value that rearranges and orders lesser values. Wars, revolutions, nationalist uprisings, killing, cheating, stealing, and deceiving in the defense, improvement, and perfection of polities are all too common to be written off as mere behavioral aberrations. Any political theory must explain this universality, and no simple instrumental conception of the polity will explain enough. People seem to behave as if they value their polity far beyond any direct, tangible good.

Thus, we must infer that the notion of a good life is inextricably tied up with the notion of life in a polity; there is little evidence that man can conceive of a good life outside or unrelated to a polity. Having suggested the primacy of the polity in all conceptions of the good life, regardless of verbal professions, we must now go on to examine some of the alternative conceptions of what characterizes a good life within polities.

Polity

Earlier in this study we postulated calculated control as a concept useful in explaining the dynamic-of-action aspect of certain types of behavior patterns. We saw that under certain conditions many people appear to respond with uniformity to certain words and actions of a determinate few, that there is also a reciprocal quality in which, under certain conditions, the determinate few respond to certain acts and words of the more indeterminate many. We have also noted that in some instances control acts and schemes appear to be undertaken pursuant to deliberation and choice, and that there is a high correlation between the prescription and the performance of discrete acts. To explain this phenomenon we postulate the existence of a process we call calculated or deliberate control. Calculated control, however, is too general and formless to serve any but the most crude and general analytical purpose. We are thus led to postulate another universal element which will account for the limits and shape of certain control patterns and which will in turn become instrumented in the process of imposing control. This element we shall call polity.

What empirical phenomena can be explained by using the concept of polity? In the first place there appears to be a certain universality in the symbolic representation, in both words and objects, of large aggregates of people. Flags, insignia, standards, and banners are universally designated to represent and characterize determinate aggregates of people. Similarly, certain aggregates are given distinctive names and distinctive qualities. The human world is divided into aggregates of people in the sense that these aggregates are distinctive and are mutually distinguishable in the manner of their symbolic representation. Whatever their independent existence as actual concrete objects, there is a unified set of distinctive symbolic representations in such words as the United States of America, Athens, or the Sioux.

Beyond symbols and symbol patterns there are other observable phenomena for which we need to account. For example, there are behavior patterns that correspond and vary with the use of symbol patterns. In wars the lining up on various sides appears ordered rather than random. Taxes are not paid to casually selected tax collectors. Disputes are not settled by uniform universal rules or random unpatterned rules, nor are they settled by uniform or random persons. People belong to, symbolically represent, and behave with reference to differentiating, determinate aggregates. These are the behavioral phenomena that must be explained both in terms of why they exist or why life is organized in this fashion, and also in terms of the processes and factors that lend continuity, stability, and dynamic qualities to the aggregates.

Calculated control acts and regularized, observable responses form distinctive patterns among people who do not know or encounter each other. Calculated control operates so as to form a unit; it operates in a distinctive fashion within that unit; and the unit itself is a distinctive part of the control process.

However, a dynamic but undifferentiated continuum of control neither reflects nor adequately explains what exists in fact, nor does it alone enable us to organize our thinking in a useful manner; [1] thus we must introduce the concept of form. Form implies structure, limits, boundaries, parameters, peripheries, margins, and patterns. It refers to regularized and stable relatedness within a set of phenomena, and the aspect that differentiates one set of phenomena from another. Form applied to action implies that certain discrete acts are pulled together and arranged, and others are separated out and disjoined. Polity is the dominant form aspect of politics, and politics takes its name from this form aspect. Affairs involving the polity are political affairs.

Further development of polity as an explanatory and analytical concept can be profitably combined with an explanation of why we use the word "polity" rather than the word "state." Although the form aspect of calculated control involving great aggregates of people has been given various names at various periods in history, the existence of a form-imparting element has remained constant. Usually the change in name has reflected some limited change in the form, but the all-important form aspect has persisted. Such words as state, republic, commonwealth, polis, principality, kingdom, union, have been and are used. We shall use the term polity to encompass all these terms and hence to refer to what we regard as the form quality common to all of them. If we were concerned only with explaining the modern period, and that only with modern concepts, we could use the term "state," but state is too culture- and time-bound. We need a concept that transcends state and serves to explain rise as well as time- and culture-bound features. By examining its nature and rise, we can show the need for a more encompassing concept, and then propose such a concept.

State was developed during a period when there was a crisis in the control of the more remote environment. In the Middle Ages and the early modern period there was a fusion and a confusion of the religious and secular, the public and the private, the empire and the kingdom, and law and custom. In order to meet this crisis in the West, a new and clear object of loyalty had to be developed, and it was in this historical context that the word "state" and its corollary, "sovereignty," came into existence.[2] The reaches of legal systems were sharply defined, the agency of rule was simplified, and obligations of loyalty were made unmistakable for all people. The basis of this loyalty was no longer simply religion or dynasty. A new object of loyalty, which incorporated the religious and the dynastic but which went beyond them, resulted from a control crisis. The new object was finally called the nation-state. But in order to serve in specific situations, the nation-state and sovereignty concepts imposed rigid distinctions which improved their normative usefulness but reduced their analytic usefulness. They assumed a definition of the sovereign power, a distinction between the legal and the customary, loyalty and disloyalty, public and private—all of which were mainly normative and not descriptive of how people lived. The state and sovereignty were discussed as ideals, not as behavior patterns. Very little attention was directed to how people in fact behaved.

That it was necessary to develop concepts less rigidly confined to so-called state activity, but encompassing underlying similarities between state activity and nonstate activity is suggested by the need to define state for particular purposes of analyses, and by the use of substitute terms. One of the earliest uses of polity in the English language, according to the Oxford English Dictionary, was in 1538 when a people was described as rude and without polity. In 1594, Richard Hooker examined the elements of rule in the Church of England in his *Laws of Ecclesiastical Polity*. Hooker clearly could not use such words as state and kingdom. He needed a word to indicate relatedness but not identity in certain aspects of state and church. He used polity: "The necessitie of Politie and Regiment in all Churches may be held, without holding any one certayne forme to bee necessary in them all. Nor is it possible that any form of politie, much less politie ecclesiasticall should be good, unlesse God himselfe bee authour of it." [3]

Despite occasional exceptions, there has been a steady narrowing and refinement of the meaning of the word "state" in modern times. The trend has been toward increasing formality in its reference, increasing normative precision in its inclusiveness and exclusiveness, and increasing rigidity in the obedience expected in its name. This trend and other concepts related to state, such as sovereignty, social contract, and *raison d'état*, developed to reduce the confusion associated with the change of governance from church and royal families to officials of the state.

These developments produced a situation in which state was either regarded as the highest or ideal form of political evolution, or as a mystical entity with overtones of divine origin. Thus state was so vested with normative content that it was not very useful for describing reality. In common usage it is a concept that is too specific, too formalistic, too rigid, too normative, and too artificial to explain politics. Moreover, we must have a theory that will explain the state before we can argue that the state explains anything.

The predominantly instrumental and fabricated character of state seems to underly a valid point made by T. D. Weldon:

> The confident and uncritical way in which 'the State' is used
> by many modern writers suggests that 'State' is the same sort

of word as 'water', 'mountain', or 'sun'. It is easy to see that this is a mistake. There is no reason to doubt that when Cicero wrote *'aqua'* *'mons'*, or *'sol'*, he was referring to things indistinguishable for practical purposes from those to which we refer by 'water', 'mountain', and 'sun'. But 'State' is not in the same way equivalent to *'respublica'* or *'civitas'*.[4]

Weldon goes on to examine some of the efforts that have been made to vest state with distinctively natural properties, which will make it refer to a determinate object just as the word "apple" does, and he finds that none of the efforts have made it a useful concept for the formation of political theories.

What we are concerned with here is why state, along with city-state, monarchy, empire, and principality, has occupied such an important place in human history.

The beginning of politics is an awareness of the more remote environment. The hypothesis advanced here is that this awareness is limited, and it deals with something that the individual knows incompletely because it is beyond his day-to-day encounters. Simultaneously structuring and trying to control the more remote environment gives rise to a polity as a necessary by-product. Aristotle was right when he said man is a political animal if he meant man is a polity-conscious animal. For the present, polity may be taken to refer to the most comprehensive social system that any individual perceives and regards himself as a member of. It is the most comprehensive interaction pattern with which a person identifies, describing his relation to it as "we" and "ours," rather than "they" and "theirs." There is a polity for virtually every individual who is aware of a world beyond the one he experiences fully. Studying or trying to control the more remote environment creates a polity both as image and as fact.

In the first place, polity refers to a determinate, shared perception, an image common to the minds of some but not all individuals. It calls attention to the form of the object. The polity image will vary between any two individuals, but it will vary within limits both in the cognized configuration that gives character to the image and in the kind and intensity of feelings evoked. Polity also specifies the form of the observed behavior: observations are shared and agreed to constitute a fact, despite the varying perceptions of different observers.

It was noted earlier that political theorists tend to identify either "power" or "state" as the essence of politics. We have tried to show that control, although related to power, is a more useful conceptualization of the active element in politics than power. However, because it leaves out the identification of the form element, we have not argued that control, or even calculated control, is the whole of politics. Power is not a sufficiently useful specification of either the active or the potential element of politics; it emphasizes the capability of action and neglects the universally important element of form. State, as generally used, specifies a form that is not universal. Those who argue that so-called state activities are the basic stuff of politics find that when their arguments are pushed to their logical conclusion they base all relevant characteristics upon form alone. It should be emphasized, however, that the concept of state is a part of the concept of politics, just as power is a partial but inadequate concept of organization.

The use of the word "polity" makes it possible to merge form and action elements into the words "politics" and "politicize." The nature, existence, and role of what we call polity must be explained and its dominant characteristics accounted for. It has been a common practice to explain politics in terms of what the state requires. In the view taken here, the order of inquiry must be reversed and the concept of state, or more generally, polity, must reflect and help explain what is observed.

Before we proceed to a separate consideration of polity as

fact and as perception, we must make clear the philosophical and scientific assumptions underlying the distinction. Two axioms are required. The first rejects the tenet of phenomenological philosophy that nothing exists except as it is perceived, that all objects are subjective. It is considered unscientific to account for large areas of agreement about phenomena by postulating coincidence of mental pictures unrelated to the objects pictured. According to the first axiom, there exists an objective, real, or factual order which is not dependent upon the existence of a human perceiver; i.e., objects may exist without subjects.

The second axiom is that the sense impressions or stimuli which act upon man as he relates to the world outside himself are mediated, sorted, and organized by a mechanism or process within himself, and hence that most of man's responses to external stimuli are not simple $S \rightarrow R$ responses but rather $S \rightarrow O \rightarrow R$ responses in which O stands for organism. Because O mediates between the stimulus and the response, different individuals may respond to the same stimuli in different ways, depending on what O contributes to the formation of the response: there may be great similarity, or verticalness as some psychologists call it, between the stimulating object and the product of O's operation, or there may be great dissimilarity, but in no case is there absolute identity. Thus it is possible to talk meaningfully about the differences in the way we see things (sight being representative of all sense stimuli as mediated or reorganized by O) and the way things are.

In much of our day-to-day experiences with the close-at-hand world the distinction between how we see things and the way things really are is of relatively little importance; on this basis we interact with our environment with a fair degree of success. Thus, there is little practical difference between the statements "That is a table" and "I see a table." But where it is very difficult or impossible to test by well-established means for differences between what is and what is seen, the importance becomes critical. There is a great practical difference between the statements "I see a Communist menace" and "There is a Communist menace." The more one deals with phenomena beyond what he is able to experience directly by his senses, by what Allport calls encounter, the more important becomes the distinction between the perception or image (the product of O) and the object as it is.[5] We are concerned with man's more remote environment and hence we are as interested in how men see their world as we are in how it really is. We must be prepared to see people act on the basis of what they see rather than upon the basis of things as they are.

There is good reason to believe that man is able to perceptualize the United States and act in accord with his perception even when he is unable fully to encounter or to conceptualize the United States. Concepts are the tools of analysis. Percepts are the basis of action. Man is required to act on the basis of his perception of the United States, much as he is required to act on the basis of his perception of an automobile. There is a growing tendency nowadays to use the term "image" to refer to objects only partly sensed. But whatever the word—perception, image, or other—we are, for the reasons set forth, interested in what Walter Lippmann has called the pictures in men's heads, and the relation between the pictures and the objects, and relatable action. It is against this background of psychology and philosophy that we turn first to a discussion of the polity as observable behavior and then to a discussion of polity as a perception or image.

How would a detached observer go about establishing the objective existence of polity as we have defined it?[6] Would the task be different from that of establishing the existence of a chair in a room? The answer is that the approach would be the same, but the operations would be different.

Polity is a distinctive type of interaction pattern. Its objective existence must ultimately be established by observation of a number of instances. There are many behavior patterns that are common to all of mankind. Communicating through language with other persons is one such pattern. Language as one characteristic ingredient of an interaction pattern only distinguishes human beings from other animals, but there are differences in language and it is possible for a detached observer to define those who share a common language. Those persons who speak and communicate through a common language can be regarded as having an objective existence, much as a chair might be thought of as having an objective existence.

In establishing the objective existence and form of an interaction pattern it is necessary to grasp the notion of behavioral boundaries. For example, to pursue the matter of language: people communicate and interact with varying degrees of effectiveness, but at some point an arbitrary line marking these degrees of effectiveness is taken to constitute a boundary. This produces a situation in which the line between those who understand and those who do not understand is blurred. We have to say in such a case that the object (the aggregate of people sharing a common language) is indeed determinate but that its separation from its environment cannot be sharply drawn. Blurred boundaries of this sort, of course, liberate the perceiving process and open the way for differences between perceivers. This creates problems of action, especially control action. Nevertheless the interaction pattern must be regarded as having boundaries and it is at the boundaries or margins that we must look for the character of the object. Now let us apply this line of reasoning to the task of establishing a polity as an objective fact.

Polity is used to refer to the most comprehensive and inclusive unit which any individual regards himself as sharing with others who are unknown but determinate.[7] It is postulated that every human being has a "we" and a "they" sense, much as he has a sense of leftness and rightness. The "we" feeling is expressed with reference to all interaction patterns where he is conscious of attachment or belonging—from "we, the family" to "we, the people of the United States" to "we, the human race." The expression "we," then, includes many people he does not know, as well as so great a number of people he could not possibly know them. All who regard themselves as part of a determinate "we" constitute a polity which can be established empirically: their number can be ascertained, the distinctive interaction pattern complex which sets them apart from other peoples can be described. These people engage in cooperative undertakings, and a boundary can be observed between those who cooperate and those who do not. The components of the "we" feeling and the "we" behavior can be dissected.

Even where there are blurred or relatively indistinct boundaries, there is a structure. At some boundaries the rate of interaction declines sharply and at others there is a qualitative difference in the focus of interaction. For example, the payment of taxes changes and those who pay at a particular rate and to a common collector constitute a distinctive aspect of the interaction pattern. A call to arms evokes a common response from certain persons and a different response from others. If we multiply acts like these many times, note the pattern development and the boundaries, the object will emerge as a concrete reality, enabling accurate prediction of what will and what will not happen. If we restrict observers to such matters, we must expect substantial convergence in their reports. People who regard themselves as citizens of Canada will not ordinarily pay taxes levied by the United States.

A polity, then, is an interaction pattern which can be observed and described. It is characterized by limited change.

It represents objective form, "objective" meaning simply that set of characteristics designated by independent observers as a common symbol and which can be checked by many observations or encounters. Only when the form or pattern has been established and agreed upon can various aspects of the pattern be measured. The problem is to define polity in such a manner that it can be identified by independent observers.

Having specified by definition what we are looking for, the next task is to suggest the kinds of evidence acceptable. To pursue this task, let us suppose that if people are concerned about their more remote environment they will endure deprivations for returns that are remote and vague. These people engage in a relation that resembles what we ordinarily call an exchange relation but which has none of the specific qualities associated with a transaction, a bargain, or a contract. For example, they pay out money or goods, and receive intangibles like security, law, or general welfare in return. Obviously what we are describing here are some of the characteristics of taxation as distinguished from the marketplace transaction.

Similarly, if people are concerned about controlling their remote environment, they will endure personal inconvenience in order to select leaders with whose qualifications they are unfamiliar. Their expectation of these people is as vague as their expectation of return from their tax dollar.

Suppose that upon investigation we find that a very high proportion of the people at all times have made sacrifices similar to those we associated with taxation, and that this practice is universal, transcending time, space, and cultures. This suggests, though it does not prove, a universal concern with what gives rise to acts to control the more remote environment.

However, it does not delineate the polity. To do this we must find through investigation that some people pay their taxes to one collector while others pay to other collectors. We must also learn that some persons pay taxes for one set of enterprises, while others pay taxes for a different set of enterprises. Furthermore we have to find that for some people the amount of the tax is determined one way, by one agency, and for other people, by other processes and agencies. If we consider all people who pay taxes to a common collector and find that these taxes are levied by the same process and by the same agencies, and used for common undertakings, and if we then draw a line between these people and all who pay to other collectors, we have begun to find a boundary as an objective fact. The line need not be drawn in territorial or spatial terms (although two people cannot occupy the same space at the same time and there are reasons for the special importance of the territorial boundary which will be examined later). What we have suggested here is a means by which one might begin to mark out the boundaries of a polity. If upon further investigation we find that within these same boundaries people voted for common leaders and officials, responded to calls to arms, rendered deference to common leaders and symbols, then we have established the internal-external dimension in such a manner that independent and detached observers could agree about the existence of the discrete object.

In addition to having boundaries that distinguish it from its environment, an object must have a distinctive internal structure which is articulated with the boundaries but is not the same thing. This involves the ordering of the internal parts or components and has been variously called the means-end dimension, the division of labor, and, by Talcott Parsons in one of his formulations, the instrumental-consummatory axis.[8] What kind of evidence can we seek to establish an instance of a distinctive internal structure which reflects or results from action to control the more remote environment? This is mainly a matter of looking for substructures of a characteristic kind.

We might reason that in order for there to be control of the more remote environment of all individuals within boundaries, which for all would be the environment across the boundaries, there would have to be certain adjustive and control acts taken in unison in the light of information about disruptive forces. There would have to be at any time a set of discrete individuals whose acts and words would in fact be deferentially responded to in certain concerns and undertakings. We say that such a leadership or authority structure has to exist because the kind of common undertakings necessary to deal with the more remote environment are inconceivable without it. We have no reason for believing that without a tax collector taxes would be paid except perhaps capriciously. We would not expect conflicts to be settled by any common rule, nor armed forces to spontaneously assemble to reduce external threats of extinction and chaos.

In order to delineate the internal substructures of the polity we have to mark out boundaries between them and find the boundaries between polity undertakings and those not relevant to polity. We would expect this boundary in any polity or there would be no polity structure distinctive from general structure. The acts relevant to dealing with the more remote environment would not exist. Where the boundary is located in any concrete polity is subject to empirical investigation. Implied here is a distinction between public officials and private persons and public processes and private processes. We could expect to find a set of polity-relevant rules which investigation should show to have causal consequences running to the boundaries of the polity, and this set of rules would be set off from rules, conventions, and practices which were not regarded as polity relevant. Thus, we would find a distinction between legal and nonlegal matters as well as between legal and illegal behavior.

It is important to be clear about what we have established when we have established a polity as an object. We have established something that is essentially static, in the sense that change is limited or operates within limits. Too much change and certain kinds of change lead either to a change in the nature of the object, much as a chair might change into a bed, or the object may dissolve into its environment and lose the character of an object. The object whose existence we have established is not a person, it has no independent life. The most we can say is that it is an object and as such it is bounded and has characteristic structural properties. We can also say that this particular object reflects the working of a purpose on the part of human beings. We can further speculate that once the object exists it can have instrumental uses. But this is only true if it is perceived as an object.

One difference between the chair and the polity recalls an earlier discussion of the difference between a percept and a concept. We noted that for there to be a percept it must be possible for the perceiver to encounter or otherwise be subject to direct sense stimuli from the object; and that where this is not possible we are dealing with the type of more exclusively mental construct generally called a concept. Certainly no one can see, touch, smell, and hear a polity completely; it is too large and too complete. Therefore its existence can only be established by a sampling procedure in which one tests for the existence of strategic or highly relevant characteristics and on the basis of these samplings concludes that the object in fact exists. But the use of this sampling procedure is not confined to establishing the objective existence of a polity. It is the common method by which we in practice learn about much of our environment, and the fact that we are able to survive and cope with that environment on the basis of sampling indicates the validity of using it. This being the case there is no reason not to consider the perceiving process as relevant to understanding and "seeing" the polity as an object. We are, however, faced with the problem of degree of difference in the way the object is and the way it is seen. We must now turn to a consideration of polity as a perception or image.

What justification is there for treating the perception or image of polity separately from polity as an object that exists and can be described without positing an observer or perceiver? In deciding upon this procedure we have been influenced by two considerations. One is simply a conviction born out of long observation and reflection that some such separation must be postulated in order to account for much of what is commonly called political behavior. The second is that the findings and theoretical development by perceptual psychologists seem to confirm or at least support the validity of this approach.

The foregoing somewhat labored effort to establish the object aspect of polity was necessary in order to differentiate and clarify the objective aspect of polity. In his work on perception, Floyd Allport suggests and in some detail describes a structuring process through which man learns about the world in which he lives, or, as Allport puts it, that man gets approximately "in tune" with the world about him.[9] As he sees it, this process consists of sensory stimuli which come only from certain points. "These points," he argues, "deriving by stimulation from the stimulus object . . . represent environment items that are capable of producing a denotive, physicalistic experience. . . . If this conjecture is correct, it is evident that perceptions are not directly or entirely given by the stimulus-objects they represent but are partly works of construction in the organism. And the 'facsimiles' that are structured by whatever processes, and that connect or fill in the point-representation of the denotable landmarks, will sometimes be close approximations of the physical object, but sometimes only 'reasonable' likenesses, and occasionally very poor."[10]

It follows from this conjecture that the fewer the denotable points the greater the latitude for the works of construction in the organism. For an individual there are relatively few denotable points about any polity. Thus the element of fill-in by the organism can be very great.

In recent times there has developed a practice of using image in somewhat the way psychologists use percept. It appears to be a kind of cross between the classic meaning of percept and concept. It is perhaps not entirely fortuitous that image in its newer usage has found most favor with political analysts and advertising agencies. The reason for this will become more evident as we go along. It is also probably no accident that the word is used by analysts who are probing the roots of human behavior and trying to effect some sensible reconciliation between the rational and irrational sides of the human species, as well as between the dichotomy of fact and value which the logical positivists have pressed upon our attention. A suggestive exploration of the image has been made by Kenneth Boulding, an economist concerned with the whole of human behavior. Boulding's *The Image* opens with this arresting passage:

> As I sit at my desk, I know where I am. I see before me a window; beyond that some trees; beyond that the red roofs of the campus of Stanford University; beyond them the trees and the roof tops which mark the town of Palo Alto; beyond them the bare golden hills of the Hamilton Range. I know, however, more than I see. Behind me, although I am not looking in that direction, I know there is a window, and beyond that the little campus of the Center for the Advanced Study in the Behavioral Sciences; beyond that the Coast Range; beyond that the Pacific Ocean.[11]

He goes on to tell how he knows he is located in space, time, personal relations, and in nature, as well as in a world of subtle intimations and emotions:

> What I have been talking about is knowledge. Knowledge, perhaps, is not a good word for this. Perhaps one would rather say

my *Image* of the world. Knowledge has an implication of validity, of truth. What I am talking about is what I believe to be
true; my subjective knowledge. It is this image that largely
governs my behavior. . . . *The first proposition of this work,
therefore, is that behavior depends on the image.*[12]

Clearly Boulding is struck by the need to explain the structuring process through which an individual seems to impose
order and form upon a world that is beyond his direct experience, just as the perceptual psychologists are struck by the
differences between the way things are and the way they are
seen. Boulding's development and widespread application of
image to phenomenon is highly suggestive, especially in the
field of social phenomena, although there is much more of
the philosophical and purely speculative treatment than there
is in the work of the perceptual psychologists as they are re-
viewed by Allport.

Having made some effort to justify the separate treatment
of polity as object and polity as percept or image and to furnish some support for the distinction, we are ready to consider
the nature of polity as a percept.

In his development of the nature of perception Allport takes
up what he calls six broad classes of perceptual phenomena.
The first four deal with directly encountered objects. They
are: sensory qualities and dimensions, figural or configurational
aspects, perceptual constants, and dimensional frames of reference. It is, however, the last two that are of special interest
to the political theorist. These Allport calls concrete object
character and the effect of the prevailing set of state:

Things and events appear to us not as mere qualities, dimensions, or forms, but as things and events. *Concrete object character* . . . is a fundamental property of practically all our
perceptions. Perhaps the most salient feature of this phenomenon is that it represents 'meaning.' The meaning that it repre-

sents, however, is not of mere configuration or wholeness of the object, not how large or bright the object is, but the experience of *what* the object is. Since events are also included in our broad definition of 'object' we can extend this aspect to include the concrete character or meaning of actions and situations.[13]

Of the concrete object character, Allport notes that it would probably be the same for all persons having a common background of experience. The effect of the prevailing set or state would, however, vary among individuals and among different states of an individual at different times.

It has long been known that particular sets of the individual, or attitudes, either long standing or momentary, affect the selection of objects that will be perceived and to some extent the readiness with which they are perceived. Phenomenologically they also result in a greater attentive clearness or vividness of those objects. To this aspect of perception the concrete-object character of the stimulus is especially relevant, for when we take the character and meaning of the object into account we can often see a relation between it and the state the individual is in. The phenomenon is most clearly shown with respect to objects that we are looking for or meanings that we are seeking to realize from stimulus-situations that are undetermined or vague. . . . Perceptual sets or readinesses induced by needs are both common and important. Emotional states may also determine perceptual readiness or the manner in which we perceive certain objects or relationships. . . . The way in which indefinite or ambiguous things are perceived may to some extent be influenced by the individual characteristics of the perceiver, a fact implied by the use of the Rorschach test for personality diagnosis. . . . We should not, however, overlook the fact that the 'set to perceive' may often be based not upon any strong motivating, emotional, or personality condition, but upon nothing more dramatic than the *frequency* and *familiarity* of the object in the observer's experience. The effects we have mentioned are usually matters of selective emphasis, determining what objects we are to perceive in our environment and what objects we are to ignore.[14]

With this background we shall now turn to a more detailed examination of polity as a perception or image.

At some point in the process of maturing an individual becomes aware of the existence of an "earthly world" that he does not directly experience or encounter. He constructs the world from information given him through word symbols and from interpretation of isolated events ordered in some fashion by his imagination and by the general process called socialization. Although he knows relatively little about this world from direct firsthand experience, he becomes accustomed to relating events in it to his firsthand experiences. For example, a man is asked to go away and fight and returns to find his wife stolen and his house burned; or he is asked to share his possessions in the form of paying taxes, and when he asks why, he is told of enemies and causes beyond his personal experience.

In short, man, through his imagination and his experience with word symbols, is able to give form and organization to the world, by combining his firsthand knowledge of his immediate world with his isolated and partial experience of the more remote world. We know something of this because of man's verbal behavior about it, and because of acts he performs based upon it. In this sense a polity is created when an individual, having become conscious of events that he does not experience fully and directly, begins to order these events so as to deal with them and to increase his psychic comfort. Thus it is that consciousness of a more remote environment, a perception or image of it, and the impulse to control and give form to it come into existence somewhat simultaneously and universally in the normal maturing mind. This is, of course, a hypothesis, but as will be shown subsequently, one that is useful in explaining a fair range of observable phenomena.

We may say then—by altering Voltaire's famous remark that if God did not exist man would have to invent him—that if the polity did not exist as an object man would have to invent it in order to order his world. The will or impulse to control the perceived but partially unknown produces the polity, because formless and undifferentiated control is unthinkable and impossible. The will or impulse to give form to the partially unknown arises simultaneously with the impulse or will to control it in accordance with the image held and the feelings stirred.

From what has been said it should be clear that there can be a rather large gap between the polity as an object and the polity as an image or percept. The individual is able to learn so little of it through his senses that there is great latitude for his own structuring process to operate. Realizing this helps explain a number of observable practices in the field of political behavior.

Because the polity's existence is only known through patterned consequences which are predictable in probability terms and which would be otherwise unexplainable, it seems natural that symbolization would play an important role in portraying its nature. This also explains why there is so much literary and metaphorical discourse about politics, which in turn helps to explain why the polity is so often personified in discourse. Kenneth Boulding has said: "It must not be thought, of course, that symbolic images are all 'bad.' Indeed, the symbolic image is absolutely necessary as a part of the economy of image formation. The human imagination can only bear a certain degree of complexity. When the complexity becomes intolerable, it retreats into symbolic images." [15]

It is very common for people, particularly politicians, political scientists, and journalists, to speak of the polity as a kind of self-directed, self-willed, and self-motivated actor. Such statements as "The state demands the loyalty of its citizenship," "The state rests its case," and "The state controls too much of the economy," are examples of the type of widely used expression. To find out how these expressions lack precision we must ask "Under what conditions is it meaningful to regard the polity as an actor analogous to an acting human being?" Objectively we may say that the polity is simply a pattern, an object, a bounded structure. The notion that polity is related to action is profoundly true, but a knee joint, a highway, and a set of instructions are also related to action. Although we may speak of these as actors metaphorically, in all cases they may be thought of as either the *result* or *object* or *condition* of action, or as pure form within which action takes place, or as descriptive of the *form* phase of action.

A polity exists when a series of predictable acts form a set or pattern of a certain kind. Once it is perceived we can attribute qualities to it in both its objective and subjective aspect. In either case, however, it is a reflection of action by human beings and is reducible to acts of individuals and predictions of such acts. A disciplined approach to discourse requires that when polity is the subject of a sentence, it never be used with any verb except *to be*. It may be the object of many verbs but should never have lifelike action qualities attributed to it.

This kind of strictness may help decrease the metaphorical content and increase the scientific content of political discourse, but it seems a bit too austere to explain events. A feeling persists that polity has a different relation to action than that of pure form, that its relation to action is not simply like that of the river banks to the flowing water. This suggests that the interplay between perceptions of polity and value systems may be constituents of a control system. For example, polity enters into control when a person is deferred to merely because he speaks in the name of the polity. The President of the United States does not have to say that he is using perception of country to get us to do something. We defer to him because he speaks in the name of the polity.

Having identified a certain kind of phenomenon, called it polity, and explained its essential nature as pattern and as instrument, we may now turn to an examination of some of the dominant characteristics of a polity, both as external object and as image, and try to account for those characteristics. The main characteristics that require explanation and theory are: territoriality, characteristic symbolic representation, and government (including law and jurisdiction).

Empirically, nearly all concrete polities seem to have territorial boundaries or what might be called territorial form. As a comprehensive interaction pattern which exists and which is perceived and sustained a polity could be conceived aside from territorial boundaries. Indeed such nonterritorial polities have existed, have been advocated and predicted. During the great migrations of the Middle Ages the political form was not predominantly territorial. Karl Marx predicted and advocated a polity based upon the structure of relations growing out of means of production, regardless of territorial location. In international relations there has developed the idea of extraterritoriality, and the notion that a polity must have contiguous territory is even now giving way to the actuality of polities with spatially separated territory. Pakistan is a case in point; Alaska and Hawaii as states are further examples. Then too we have the British Commonwealth of Nations and the rise of such entities as NATO, the Organization of European States, and the like. To be sure these latter involve territorial boundaries, but their development seems to suggest that even empirically any concrete polity is less dependent upon particular kinds of territorial boundaries.

Another fact should be noted to clarify the relation between object and perception: the territorial boundaries of a polity can be changed without creating a new polity. As a polity, the United States was not changed by the acquisition or admission of Alaska and Hawaii. Germany was still Germany with and without Alsace and Lorraine. The more radical altering of boundaries such as the present division into East and West Germany presents a different problem, but even here the territorial division has been accompanied by other changes in the interaction pattern and a slow developing of new perceptions. The point is that any territory with boundaries is not a polity, and that a polity can undergo boundary changes without bringing into existence a new polity, especially a new perception of a polity.

Although it is possible to show that neither in thought nor in experience is territorial definition an imperative for the existence of a polity, the fact remains that territoriality has played, and seems destined to continue playing, an extraordinarily important part in the life of polities. We must ask why this is so.

Territoriality has the very great virtue of simplifying enormous complexity and of providing a few denotable points. More perhaps than any other representation of a polity, a map is thought to be like the country in a sense that a flag or a name is not. Bounded space is so familiar that grasping this nature or aspect of an object gives a comforting sense of a real object with which to identify. Another virtue of the territorial aspect arises from the requirement that a control system have clearly and generally understood boundaries. Drawing a line in what would otherwise be undifferentiated space, and saying that all persons on one side of the line are a "we" in relation to the "they" or "theys" on the other side greatly facilitates the process of control. It clarifies so that everyone can understand who is required to do what. There is indeed a kind of universality about the use of territorial boundaries in control systems of all kinds, as indicated by the territorial subunits within polities, and also by their use in the whole range of organized human activity.

Another observable characteristic of polities is the extent of their symbolic representation and the distinctive nature of that representation. Except for religion, no interaction pattern is so extensively represented by symbols, rituals, and ceremonies. And in a fundamental sense, there is a great similarity between symbolic representations of all polities. Mere mention of the more obvious ones makes the point clear. Polities have flags, staffs, seals, investiture ceremonies, titles, oaths, protocol, badges, uniforms, songs, personifications, maps, and forms of address. If polities are compared with other interaction patterns, such as family, business, trade associations, and labor unions, the difference in the amount and type of symbolic representation may be readily seen. The reason for a great amount of symbolic representation in religious activity is essentially the same as for politics, as will be shown.

How do we explain this large amount of symbolism in connection with polities? Again we have to go back to those activities about which we know and develop a concern but which we do not personally and directly experience. Any word is a symbol in a basic sense. It is one thing that stands for another thing. The word "nail," for example, is a symbolic representation of a particular object that can be understood apart from its symbol. Misunderstandings that arise because of different symbols for the same object can rather readily be cleared up by picking up the object and showing it. We would expect, however, that as the difficulty of direct referral to the object increased, the independent importance of the symbol would also increase, and that a set of symbols would develop that stood for events-objects that could not be readily and fully experienced directly. In order to communicate about such matters it is necessary to have many unreferrable under-standings expressed by a single symbol.[16] Control involves communication, and the more difficult it becomes to explain verbally the ends and means of control, the more reliance there must be upon people's attachment to, and investiture of, the symbols themselves. Symbolic representation plays an impor-tant role in politics because feelings and respect for the sym-bols themselves must be inculcated if communications are to evoke the intended response. The complexity and unknow-ability of the polity, even if it is sharply bounded as a territory, explains why discourse about it is so highly dependent upon symbols with distinctive qualities. What are those distinctive qualities and how are they explained?

The characteristic political symbols are largely nonverbal. They are simple and have little or no intrinsic value. In any polity some of them have unusual evocative capacity and great effort is expended to facilitate their acceptance. The flag is probably the model political symbol. Think how much it com-municates and yet how difficult it would be to produce the phenomenon to which it refers. Like territorial boundaries it is a great simplifier. What it expresses cannot be converted into its referent; it cannot even be converted into word sym-bols. What we are saying here is that all polities are symboli-cally represented to a large extent, and that although each tends to develop its own distinctive symbols, the differences between polity symbols and nonpolity symbols are greater than the differences between symbols of different polities.

The third characteristic of a polity is a government, and all that a government implies in the way of law and jurisdiction. How does a political theory explain the universal existence of a government or governmental system in each identifiable polity? In the sense that for every individual there is a polity, it is universal and timeless. But any particular polity must be accounted for empirically. A polity, for example, will always be finite or limited and will usually be bounded territorially, although the precise boundaries will be man-made. As a polity more clearly shapes increasingly complex types of control it becomes correspondingly more important for its boundaries and its symbolization to become precise and commonly known, and distinctive from other polities. It becomes more important to distinguish clearly between polity and nonpolity matters. Man takes what he finds in nature and perfects or improves it for his own use. This is what happens when precise boundaries are established by negotiation, force, or decree. It is a little like taking iron ore found in nature and imposing a useful form on it.

In addition to boundaries, however, a polity must have an internal structure which reflects both the universal structural characteristics of human interaction as well as the structural requirements imposed by the control function. When people interact there emerges identifiable role differentiation or division of labor, one of these role types being what we call leadership. Moreover, common understandings develop about many matters such as priorities, precedence, the permitted and forbidden. Finally there emerge groupings of related roles which produce what might be called a structure of groups. These three—leadership, common understandings, and specialized groups—may be thought of as the natural or inevitable consequences of complex interaction, wherever it is found. But like the boundaries of a polity, these must be modified if they are to be used instrumentally and intentionally by man for control purposes within the polity.

A government in a polity is nothing more than the deliberate modification of leadership so that it becomes official, of understandings so they become laws, and of groups so that they become organizations or agencies. Since the exact boundaries of any polity are not predetermined, the structure that maintains the boundaries and uses the polity for control must likewise have a determinate but varied character, but only in terms of precise structure. As government develops, leaders and functionaries come to be assigned more sharply defined roles whose performance is not dependent upon whim or accident. Understandings must be made explicit and they must extend to the boundary of the polity, thus the basic importance of jurisdiction in a legal system and in a polity. Natural units of association that arise because certain people are performing related tasks must be given an explicit structure and function. There is no greater probability that natural association will produce a controlled and regulated more remote human environment in an arbitrarily bounded polity than there is that a bunch of trees will naturally turn into a suitably designed home. A useful and viable polity, by its nature and by the very forces that brings it into existence, requires a government. And the more elaborate and complex the control purposes in the polity, the more elaborate and complex the governmental system that operates it. The natural boundaries of a polity may be used for purely descriptive purposes, both of objective interaction patterns and for perceptions of polity, the limits of concern or consciousness; but to convert this natural entity into instruments of calculated control, more precise form must be imposed upon nature by human effort. And since the precise boundaries are not natural they will not be maintained or used without deliberate direction and design.

Observation strongly suggests that calculated control is a selective process. However, it is also a process that indicates some convergence in preferences among many people. The problem of the theorist is to account for, and suggest the nature of, the ordering principle that produces the convergence. This leads to a discussion of what we call *the good polity.*

What can it mean to say of a polity, society, or state that it is good? Since this is an inquiry into causal theory it is the causal not the moral aspect of the notion of a good polity that will be examined. There seems to be a rather universal practice of vesting polities with essentially evaluative qualities. These evaluations tend to attribute either moral or aesthetic qualities to polities, much in the same way that such qualities are attributed to human beings. For example: "My country 'tis of thee, sweet land of liberty" or "Oh! Beautiful for spacious skies."

Moral and aesthetic criteria are attributed to two aspects of the polity. Either actually existing polities are characterized as being good or bad, beautiful or ugly; or goodness and beauty are treated as ideals. These criteria represent a vision of what ought to be and are properly regarded as goals to be achieved. "We the people of the United States, in order to form a more perfect union," may be taken as an aesthetic ideal, and "a new nation, conceived in liberty, and dedicated to the proposition that all men are created equal," as an ethical ideal.

Polity has been conceptualized as either an actual object or as a perception whose main importance lies in its use as an instrument. The object aspect rests upon identification and description of interaction patterns. The conception of polity as shaping behavior, however, rests upon a perception or image of the polity held by the individuals involved in the control process. But the mere holding of an image does not affect behavior. It must somehow enter into action. This raises the question of how and when an image of a polity can be used for control purposes. And the answer seems to be only when importance is attached to the image and when there is a desire to make the external world conform to the image. Thus if an individual cherishes his image of his country and pays taxes because he wants to make that country stronger, then we can say the polity, as polity, modifies his behavior. Similarly, if an individual attaches immorality or ugliness to a polity, this image may influence him to fight its armies. It is by stirring feelings and shaping cognitions that polities enter into control. This explains in a preliminary fashion why the notion of a good polity is useful. It was noted earlier that for every mature individual there is a polity. Now perhaps we should amend this to say that for every individual there is both a good polity and probably a bad polity or polities.

It goes without saying that the stronger an individual's attachment to a polity, the more it is capable of shaping his behavior. One of the paradoxes in this matter, especially in a country like the United States, is that although verbally the polity is regarded simply as a means, in order for it to be a factor in control it has to be treated as an end, something that is loved, cherished, and sustained even at great cost and sacrifice.

Wherever the existence of a polity can be established it is fair to assume that it is regarded by many people within it as a good polity, regardless of any moral or aesthetic speculation or evaluation of specific patterns. But polities are not evaluated simply in general terms, or on the basis of familiarity. Different attributes are assigned, both by specifying the virtues and vices of the polity and by expressing ideals to be striven for. Thus it becomes important to examine some of the qualities assigned and ideals sought to discover the consequences that result from different evaluations and ideals.

First, let us explore some of the essentially aesthetic evaluations. The polity that is perceived in aesthetic terms produces different consequences than one perceived in ethical terms. Take for example the difference between a good polity perceived as one that is stable, and a polity perceived as one that is just. In the name of enhancing stability, people can be asked to avoid behavior that would tend to disrupt established patterns of relations. Troublemakers, insurgents, radicals, innovators, can be condemned on the grounds that they are destroying the beauty and tranquility of the polity. People of different races, cultures, or religions may be condemned as being offensive to a particular aesthetic view of the polity.

Despite the fact that he called it justice, Plato's notion of the good polity in *The Republic* was essentially an aesthetic one, just as Socrates' argument as to why he should not escape the poison hemlock was largely an aesthetic argument.

When the good polity is perceived as being just, there is implied a desirable quality in human relations, and the consequences for the individual are the ultimate concern. An argument for helping the needy will be strengthened among those who believe that the good polity is a just polity, and this kind of polity can be converted into instruments that facilitate securing the appropriate kind of control. Abraham Lincoln, as spokesman for the United States polity, was appealing to those who perceived the good polity as merciful when he said, "With malice toward none, with charity for all." Interestingly enough Lincoln's explicit reason for fighting the Civil War was not so much justice for the Negroes, as it was the pursuit of an aesthetic ideal of union, which may have had a wider appeal than the ethical component of the good polity.

In all images of a good polity there is both an aesthetic and an ethical component and the two are never wholly isolated from one another. Therefore the exact composition must always be determined empirically. The important point is that there are different notions of what constitutes goodness in the polity, and that these differences will have different results when the image of the polity is used to exercise control.

From the viewpoint of theoretical politics, the most important questions are, what is the extent to which any polity is regarded as good or bad by those who perceive it, and what are the attributes of goodness and badness. What actually exists in practice makes very little difference. Nevertheless a question does remain as to what specifically is evaluated when goodness or badness is assigned to a polity. One way to find out about the perceived structure of a polity is to find out whose acts and states of being are regarded as the acts and being of the polity. The perception and the object perceived always seem to be related, if only tenuously.

An act, a set of acts, or a pattern of acts performed by a person or persons generally recognized as the spokesmen for the polity may be evaluated as good when judged by a distinctive set of criteria. The acts may be judged as ethically good if they involve notions of good and bad. When equality is an ethical good, acts that treat persons as equals will be judged morally good and the polity will thus be judged as good. Acts may be judged aesthetically good if they conform to some aesthetic standard. In such instances clean streets or trains running on time or soldiers marching in perfect rhythm may contribute to a characterization of the good polity. Likewise, aesthetic judgments may be based upon such characteristic symbolic representations as flags, songs, and public buildings.

An individual may become aware of interaction patterns and habits that are distinctive in his polity in comparison with patterns or habits in other polities, as he perceives them to exist there. A favorable comparison of the patterns of his polity may be the basis of his considering his polity to be good. Here again the patterns may be judged good on the basis of their ethical qualities or their aesthetic qualities. For example, the practice of not depriving a person of life, liberty, or property without due process of law may be valued because of its fairness and justice. Or a person might be influenced in his judgment by the beauty of pageants, by customs and traditions which he regards as traditional with the people, or by the characteristic music or art of the polity.

An individual may also be impressed with the verbal or

other symbolic expressions of recognized spokesmen, official or nonofficial. If Lincoln's utterances in his second inaugural come to be regarded as representative of the polity, and if the ethical sentiments of charity and tolerance and forgiveness are appealing, then the polity may be regarded as good because of its identification with such sentiments. Or one might think that Lincoln at Gettysburg eloquently expressed the underlying beauty of the polity. These expressions, of course, may be regarded as good or beautiful after being measured against independent criteria of morals or aesthetics, or they may be regarded as good or beautiful *because* they were uttered by a spokesman for a polity already regarded as good and beautiful. But more of this possibility later.

An individual may also come to attribute goodness to a polity because he has been socialized to attribute goodness to certain symbolic or mythical representations of the polity. The flag, flag ceremonies, oaths, pledges, national songs, personifications (Uncle Sam, John Bull, etc.), legends, myths, folktales, and similar phenomena may become associated with certain ethical standards attributed to the polity, or they may become vested with intrinsic qualities more in the nature of an aesthetic appeal. To say that an individual may be taught from childhood that these symbols have some kind of goodness does not explain how they came to be vested with goodness in the first place. Such vesting should be regarded as a process in which the cumulative effect is of paramount importance. Because the polity comes into existence with life itself these symbolic representations always exist for an individual.

Something of the basic process involved may be seen best when a person changes polities and is required to exchange one set of symbolic representations for another set. This process should be studied empirically. One might guess that studies would show that characterization of the polity as good would precede and determine the attributing of goodness to symbols.

This is so despite the fact that immigrants often are more careful and ostentatious in paying homage to the conventional symbols, probably because they want to give assurance that they have forsaken the old attachment and adopted the new.

In the course of a lifetime most individuals interact with persons they do not "know," in the sense of calling one another by name. This involves a certain personal familiarity and identification as distinguished from role identification. It is hard to see how feelings of goodness and badness about the persons one knows can be projected onto the polity, but an individual's evaluation of persons with whom he interacts but does not know may be based on the attributing of goodness to the polity. When people travel, for example, they interact with many people they do not know. Americans traveling through their own country often voice such sentiments as, "These Americans are great people," "Where else in the world would you find strangers so honest and kind?" "We Americans are certainly healthy and good looking in all parts of the country." Personal experience, of course, may lead to the opposite conclusions. But, it must be admitted, in the face of unpleasant personal experiences it is still possible for an individual to persist in attributing goodness to the polity. It is obvious that this matter of the basis for attributing goodness to a polity is a most complex matter. The persistence of a Negro, for example, in attributing goodness to the United States despite the unpleasantness he probably encounters in travel is an example of a polity's power of attraction. It is also interesting to note how latent feelings of goodness in the polity are brought to the surface in foreign travel. People from one polity in another polity will be attracted to each other in much the same way that people who share any common good are attracted to each other.

From what has been said it seems quite possible for a person to vest a polity with qualities of goodness in the absence of any confirming personal experience and even in the face of experiences that might be expected to lead to the opposite conclusion. In view of these factors we are led to explain two important observations: the tendency to attribute goodness to a polity in the absence of any observable basis for the characterization, and the fact that people do forsake one polity and adopt another.

Again studies need to be made in this area, but it is quite possible that, despite appearances to the contrary, both are explained by the same kind of attachment. There is some evidence to indicate that those who leave one polity for another do not do so on the basis of personally unpleasant experience or on the basis of reasoned denunciation of their original polity. People do leave one polity on the basis of the anticipation of unpleasant experience, as many Jews left Germany under Hitler. However, the number of Jews who could have left and did not is not known. Aside from persons who are deliberately persecuted *in the name of a polity,* as in Germany, it is quite clear that many persons forsake a polity without any assurance that their personal situation will be improved. This suggests that it is possible for a person to vest a different polity with goodness or betterness in the absence of compelling personal experience. This in turn suggests the importance of expectations in the perception of and attraction to a polity. This element of expectation may also explain the tendency of people to persist in vesting their polity with effectiveness, even when personal experience provides no basis for doing so. An attack by foreigners is made to appear to threaten a polityless existence which is unbearable. In a revolution or civil war, the revolutionists fight against what they perceive as the impending doom of the polity, and the opponents of the revolution fight against the same thing. This brings us to a consideration of the relation between the notion of the good life and the good polity.

From what has been said above one might conclude that there is no relation between one's perception of the good life and one's perception of the good polity. What should be said is that the relation is not simple and obvious. This is to say that there is a relation, but it is one that needs to be explored and not simply taken for granted as we might take for granted that good deeds add up to a good man, or that good features add up to a handsome man or a beautiful woman. What do we ordinarily expect to happen when an individual's notion of the requirements of the good life clash with his notion of the requirements of a good polity? In most cases we expect him to reconcile the two in some way. We expect to hear him talk about duty, the future, the common good, a higher and wider loyalty, and the like. However, when the need is great we do expect him to set aside his notion of the requirements for the good life in favor of the requirements of the good polity; if this were not done there would be no polity as a tangible object. It is true that persons who are polity conscious have been conditioned or socialized into a predisposition to reconcile, and that the social pressures to prefer the requirements of the good polity are great. The preference for polity may be buried deep in the unconscious, but somewhere there appears to be a recognition that a polity is a necessity and that questions of good and bad proceed from there. The reason a person will in the final analysis give up doing what he regards as meeting a requirement of the good life in order to support the polity is that neither he nor anyone else knows much about what will destroy the polity. When one is threatened by destruction for want of food, he knows exactly what he needs to preserve himself. Generally speaking, he also knows when he has had enough; he can readily calculate how much food it will take to sustain him for a specified period of time. Not knowing what is required to sustain the polity, he tends to resolve most doubts on the conservative side.

A controller who makes an appeal for people to set aside their personal pursuits and values in order to sustain the polity need not be regarded as hypocritical or cynical, although there is always an opportunity for him to be so. When we say that he bears, or shares in bearing, a special burden of responsibility we mean that we expect him to preserve the polity as a kind of a special assignment. If he has insight and understanding he knows something of the complex psychic forces that demand and sustain a polity, and above all he knows that there are forces of nature, so to speak, at work that he and others understand only dimly. When food supply is threatened people tend to hoard; that is, they try to avoid taking chances. If the polity is threatened controllers avoid taking chances, and they use control by asking others not to take chances. Thus, vesting of the polity with certain needs adds to its effectiveness and its preservation.

Is it possible for a person to regard the life he lives as the good life and at the same time to regard his polity as a bad polity? It seems unlikely. For one thing to regard one's polity as being bad usually means to regard another polity as good or better. Otherwise to think of one's own polity as bad is to regard it as tending toward disintegration—that is, disintegration in terms of a notion of what a polity should be. It is hard to imagine that an individual could regard living in this condition as the good life.

We have noted earlier that the concept of the good life ranks individual values. What can we say in this same context about the concept of the good polity? We can say that the good-polity image evaluates good-life notions. We can also say that a notion of the good polity is simply an instrument for the achievement of the good life. We do know that in practice it would be difficult for one act to be regarded as at once contributing to the making of a good life and being destructive of a good polity. It is not as hard to imagine one act being disruptive of the good life of an individual but at the same time essential to the preservation of a good polity. This brings us to the old question posed by Aristotle: can a man be a good man and a poor citizen, or can he be a bad man and a good citizen? Despite our contemporary rejection, at the intellectual level, of what we regard as totalitarian qualities of the Platonic and Aristotelian city-state, at the behavioral level it appears that they may have had a better understanding of deep and complex psychic forces than we are generally willing to admit. For the truth seems to be that a person cannot regard himself as a good man but a bad citizen, and that neither his contemporaries nor any controller would so regard him. And perhaps Aristotle and the Greeks were right in regarding politics, ethics, and aesthetics as being linked by nature and not by man.

What lengths man will go to in order to achieve a polity that he can regard as good is indicated by the so-called nationalism that is now sweeping much of the world. This nationalism is moving people in a degree and in a way paralleled only by religion. It is perhaps relevant to note that the religions that have been great movers of men have been those with pronounced ethical content. The attachment to a perceived good polity appears to be one of the great and distinctive movers of men. It would be superficial to regard this as simply a bit of twentieth-century madness. When people perceive a threat to the polity they affect and vest with goodness, or when the ideal component of their perception of polity changes, they can be brought en masse to protect or perfect those features which represent what they believe to be the true character of their good polity.

This all leads on to the question of whether there can be any reasoned explanation for man's propensity to give up so much in order to preserve his polity. Any political theory must make every attempt to explain why the preservation and protection of polities is regarded as a supervalue, or a dominant element of the good life. In his opinion in the Dennis case, which upheld the law restricting the Communist Party, Chief Justice Vinson made this arresting remark: "Overthrow of the Government by force and violence is certainly a substantial enough interest for the Government to limit speech. Indeed, this is the ultimate value of any society, for if a society cannot protect its very structure from armed internal attack, it must follow that no *subordinate* value can be protected" (italics added).[17] As has been suggested, behavior almost universally confirms the Chief Justice's estimate of what value is ultimate and what values are subordinate. It is seldom, in the United States at least, that we get such a clear statement of reality in this matter from a high government official.

In order to explain why the polity ranks so highly as a value one must suggest some underlying reasons, and the basis of support for the defense of such value must be found in the individual. In the final analysis, there must be a psychological explanation. The following explanation is advanced tentatively. Within himself an individual has two psychic needs that are essential to his existence and preservation. The first we shall call freedom, independence, or autonomy, and the second we shall call necessity, dependence, or support. The two needs are often represented as antagonistic or mutually exclusive, but this is not true. They are actually complementary and are best thought of as being the opposite ends of a linear scale, with the individual's needs lying somewhere along the scale indicating a combination of independence and dependence. No individual ever aspires, either verbally or behaviorally, to complete independence or freedom with all of its concomitant risk, loneliness, and anxiety. Nor does any individual ever aspire to complete dependence or submission to necessity with the dissolution of the ego that it involves. This is to say that neither freedom nor dependence can be regarded as independent values or supervalues. Only as each stands in a certain relation to the other does it represent a value. As a set we may say they are the components of an independent value based upon a profound and universal need whose fulfillment leads man to subordinate many other values often verbally given a higher ranking.

It is suggested that the existence of a polity, both as an image and as an objective fact, reflects the underlying existence of a viable or tolerable balance or equilibrium between individual independence and dependence, and between cooperative and competitive behavior. The polity seems to represent for the individual a comprehensive certainty, and thus it assures him that forces beyond control will not destroy a total adjustment between independence and dependence and cooperation and competition. If this is true, then the maintenance of the polity and an individual's relation with it is simply an indirect way of pursuing the good life in the form of its irreducible requirements and components.

An individual's polity tends to be, for him, a good and beautiful polity. Because this is so, the preservation of his polity will take precedence over the preservation of the so-called lesser associations, such as the family and the firm. Thus families willingly send members off to risk their lives fighting wars for the sake of the polity.

The explanation advanced here as to why the protection of the polity is close to the protection and the pursuit of the good life for an individual suggests an answer to the question of why treason is universally regarded as a supercrime. It also suggests a study of emigration, people forsaking attachment to one polity in order to adopt another. The hypothesis advanced here suggests that people leave a polity and adopt another when they sense potential disintegration of the polity. Too much freedom makes any individual an outcast; too much dependence makes him a slave. In either case, if he has no hope of improving his life, he should be tempted to move in the direction of a more tolerable balance.

If the polity and the good polity were simply ordinary instruments of control they would be so treated. They are not, however, and the polity to which goodness is attributed must be regarded as a basic concept of polities and indeed of life itself.

We are now in a position to return to the active or dynamic element in politics, which we have called control, and to consider the basis of the deliberate and selective control of man over man and the special applicability of each means of control to control in, over, and through a polity. This is the activity that we call politics.

TWO

Basic
Methods
of Control

Discrete, comprehensive control systems go beyond reflecting control when any set of actions has a common orientation to the control system. One basic function of the control system is to impose form on behavior, and a second basic function is to furnish an ordering principle which arranges choices according to a hierarchy of preferences. The basic political problem is to develop a system which, in maintaining its form, makes it possible to relate specific choices to the good life and facilitates action to fulfill those choices. In relating form (polity) to substance (good life), there is no reason to believe that the most appropriate interplay of the two will come about naturally. Each is essential to the other, yet each can be destructive to the other. The art of politics consists in simultaneously safeguarding each, maximizing the constructive elements of each and minimizing the destructive ones. This requires deliberate control action and appropriate responses. Deliberate control action is a technical task and produces specialization.

We call this specialization political leadership, which tends to develop its own institutions and to constitute a kind of political leadership subsystem. The formal aspect of this subsystem is generally called government.

Calculated or deliberate control within a perceived unit of more remote environment is possible only if there are methods for imposing such control. This brings us to a consideration of relevant methods by which some persons can affect the behavior of other persons. It should be emphasized that this discussion does not purport to be an enumeration and explanation of all methods by which some persons affect other persons deliberately. Rather it is confined to those which are especially related to control of the more remote environment.

All responses to deliberate control acts are viewed here as being initiated in the same way, that is, by producing discomfort in the respondent which causes him to act to reduce the discomfort. John Dewey used the word "impulse" to characterize what he regarded as the initiator of action. The hypothesis of discomfort is not unlike Dewey's impulse, but it is specifically designed to characterize what deliberately triggers an intended responsive act. From this perspective, then, differences in control methods may be viewed basically as differences in the discomfort produced, and these methods may be rated in terms of intensity of discomfort. The hypothesized intensity of the discomfort, however, must be determined by observable differences in some quality of the response acts. There may be differences in time elapsed, in certainty, and in persistence of the behavioral change.

In terms of degrees of discomfort caused, with everything else remaining equal, we put, largely by experience, coercion at one end and scientific proof at the other end of a discomfort scale. We place persuasion on the scale between terroristic violence and scientific proof. There is, however, a decline in the intensity of discomfort produced as distance increases between controller and respondent. Moreover, the methods that cause the most intense discomfort in terms of timing and certainty of response decline most rapidly in effectiveness in the face of increasing remoteness. Thus where there is great remoteness one would expect to find the effect of terroristic violence greatly diminished in producing evidence of discomfort, persuasion less diminished, and proof still less diminished.

Thus each of the methods specified represents a segment, blurred near its extremities, on an intensity-of-discomfort scale and for convenience each may be regarded as a method of control. Each may, in turn, be scaled for changing discomfort as spatial, functional, and temporal distance develops between the intended control act and responsive behavior modifications.

To sum up the approach by taking the perspective of the controller, we may say that as he contemplates his control problem he has an end in view which requires others to modify the behavior which would be expected of them if no new element were introduced into the situation. In order to modify behavior he may produce the most intense discomfort by using terroristic violence, or he may decide to use scientific proof, with its relatively mild discomforts, to effect the behavior change. But regardless of which means the controller chooses, he will also have to consider his own capacity for inflicting discomfort, and here he will have to give thought to, among other things, the proximity-remoteness factor. In short, he will have to understand the limitations of each means of control and also the methods of combining them.

The use of coercion, persuasion, and proof as means of control may be somewhat clarified by comparing them with other means that have been suggested. In an article entitled "Approaches to the Study of Political Power," [1] Franz Neumann speaks of three basic methods at the disposal of the power group. They are persuasion, material benefits, and violence. What he calls material benefits are incentives and are better considered as a form of persuasion. Persuasion, as we shall see, is characterized by the use of incentives or appeals which produce the desired modifications indirectly or as a by-product. Neumann omits proof as a means of control but he seems to incorporate it in persuasion. Proof, however, is highly specialized and is based upon a distinctive type of discomfort.

In another article, Alfred Hofstadter discusses Goethe's reflection upon the constitution of society and attributes to the great German poet and thinker the notion that there are three powers controlling the world: wisdom, force, and *Schein*. *Schein*, the author argues, is impossible to translate, but in general terms it means shining, light, illusion, fiction, duplicity, and ambiguity. Beauty is its climax: "Schein is the sum total of all ideal images and symbols which direct, guide and give meaning to social conduct." [2] *Schein* is related to what is here called persuasion. In the chapters that follow distinctions will be developed, but for the moment we may observe that there seems to be some agreement upon a trinity and that differences are not radically divergent.

4

Coercion

One man knocks another man senseless, and the senseless man gives up all of his money without offering any resistance. This is a rather strange way of describing the events. Ordinarily in a situation of this sort we would say that one man knocked another senseless and robbed him of all his money. However, by saying the senseless man gives up his money, we call attention to the consequences of the combined control act and response. This helps to clarify the mysterious variable we call control in interpersonal relations. To be even more explicit, we are led to invent the concept of control when one person does something, and another person appears to modify his normally expected behavior. Thus we see that inherent in the very idea of behavior modification is the notion of change *from* something as well as *to* something. In the most general sense we are trying to account for the behavioral changes of some people by attributing causal properties to the actions of other people in what we call a control relation. An integral part of accounting for a modification is a knowledge of the state of being prior to the specified change. But we can never know with certainty what the action would have been without the intervention of a control act, just as we can never be sure what part of the so-called new act is a result of the control act.

In the preceding illustration we assume that because he does not resist, the man has been knocked senseless. Of course, if we actually witnessed this episode, we would probably find it difficult to tell whether the man was senseless or feigning unconsciousness; but in terms of consequences of the whole control relation it does not really make any difference. The point is that we find something so unusual, so unexpected, that to explain it, we quickly conclude the robber got the money because the man was knocked senseless. Similarly, if we see a person holding up his hands while another searches his pockets, we naturally assume he is being threatened with a gun, for we would find it very hard to believe a man would offer no resistance without such persuasion. To conceive these relations in control terms we must keep in mind the difference between what we ordinarily expect and what we actually witness, and we must try to establish the part played in this modification by the action of a controller.

The foregoing illustrations introduce what we shall call the coercion hypothesis, which in turn gives rise to the idea of coercion as a distinctive method by which one person controls a part of the behavior of another person. The unexpectedness of certain behavior is such that we are led to investigate and categorize the method used to effect it. We are led to think in terms of certain kinds of behavior modifications induced in a distinctive way. According to the coercion hypothesis, the more radical changes between normally expected behavior and observed behavior are produced when a person tries to escape or cope with extreme discomfort, or when he is rendered senseless. The relationship between types of behavior modification and acute discomfort suggests that some modifications are accounted for by the acute discomfort one person produces in another, for certain specified behavioral changes are required to alleviate the acutely discomforting state. Thus, the coercion hypothesis is used to account for certain ordered changes and can, in the context of control, be thought of as the basis of the coercion method of control. In our recognition and identification of the coercion method of control we always depend on a difference between expected behavior and unexpected actual behavior. We often say unexpected behavior *must* be caused by coercion because we cannot find any other explanation for it.

The use of coercion as a method of control is generally regarded as a last resort, the ultimate means of eliciting desired behavioral changes in other persons. Thus we can expect that a method capable of radically altering behavior would be used for purposes of control. Since politics is an aspect of control we should expect there to be a relation between coercion and politics. That there is such a relationship is obvious to all students of politics. Indeed there are theories of politics that hold that coercion is the distinguishing characteristic of politics, and that all other features can be derived from it. Later on we shall examine the validity of this theory, but for the moment the main point is that coercion as a method of control needs to be examined in any theory of politics.

In order to understand the basic nature of coercion as a method of political control we must make clear the use of coercion for control in interpersonal relations before we show how it is limited and adapted in politics.

There are two steps in the use of coercion to control. First, the controller must induce in the respondent a severe discomfort, one that the respondent is extremely anxious to escape or alleviate. Second, he must convince the respondent that the only way to alleviate the discomfort is to comply with a course of behavior prescribed by the controller. For coercion to be effective the respondent must believe that this course of behavior is his only possible means of relief.

How is severe discomfort induced? The controller may lead the respondent to expect injury, either to himself or to objects he considers directly essential to his integrity or well-being. These objects include those necessary to his physical survival as well as those giving him direct support mentally and physically. The immediate family is an example of the human object type for which injury or the prospect of injury often produces acute discomfort. The degree of discomfort the controller can produce varies proportionately with the reality and severity of the prospective injury he can create in the mind of the respondent. In addition, different types of perceived injuries produce different kinds and degrees of discomfort.

States of being are ranked as increasingly desirable and increasingly painful. All people seek the former and avoid the latter. Though all people are not aware of it, a philosophy of the good life is reflected in their instinctive behavior under various conditions or in the choices they make.

It is implicit in what has been said that the degree of discomfort induced depends as much on the respondent's personality as it does on the act of the controller. This arises out of individual differences about desirable and undesirable states of being. Certain states of being are considered highly desirable and others as extraordinarily painful. There is universal agreement about matters that concern the individual's physical and psychological self. Where actual objects are concerned, opinions are more varied: an object that is meaningful to the people of one culture may be unimportant to those of another. However, regardless of these differences, some acts by controllers will generally cause acute discomfort.

There is no reason to reject the old saying that self-preserva-

tion is the first law of nature. Most people value self-preserva-
tion above all else; the most painful thoughts are those of
nonbeing or death. Intense and prolonged physical pain is
also fearful to contemplate. In all of these, discomfort is intensified by the uncertain, the unknown. Apparently the prospect of a situation he cannot cope with without forewarning
produces fear and discomfort in man.

Acute discomfort can also be produced by the threat of
social disapproval. Most individuals depend upon some approval to maintain self-identity. The possibility of loss of approval creates a great discomfort, which can be used for control purposes.

These then are some of the possible changes in states of
being that the controller must make clear to the respondent.
But it is one thing to induce acute discomfort by threats and
assaults and another thing to convert the discomfort into the
base of a control system. This brings us to the second step.

In order to convert discomfort into control, the respondent
must be made to believe that the controller's prescriptions are
his only source of relief; this limits the situations in which
coercion is a feasible method of control. Then, unless conform-
ing causes greater discomfort, the respondent will most likely
comply with the controller's rules of action.

We say that a coercive control act forces a choice in which
the alternatives available to the respondent are drastically reduced and tightly held by another person. Coercion produces
the most painful effects when both alternatives are highly undesirable. But control depends upon ranking them.

The distinguishing characteristics of the coercion hypothesis
to explain some aspects of control will be clarified as we examine other hypotheses. It should be clear, however, that what
we call coercion has great potential effectiveness against individual respondents in situations where a radical modification
is sought. It is also distinguished by the extent to which it re-

duces the will of the respondent in the process of control. It is the method that causes us to say that one person *made* another person do something against his will. All other methods of control allow for much more interplay between the controller and the respondent and a corresponding involvement of the respondent's will and reason.

It should be clear from what has been said that coercion as a method is a matter of psychic manipulation. It includes the physical dimension because the more intense discomforts generally involve physical proximity between immediate controller and respondent, and the limiting of alternative means of alleviation requires that the controller be able to foreclose all alternative methods. This often involves physical custody of the respondent. Thus we might say that coercion for control is a manipulation of the psyche but that some manipulation requires utilizing the physical.

Control is always a matter of future or prospective actions, and thus any control act is designed to affect future behavior in a determinate and predictable way. There is often some confusion about this when penalties like imprisonment and execution are used. To kill a man does not control him, it annihilates him. Killing may facilitate the control of others through psychological impact but it does not secure the compliance of the dead man. Aside from rehabilitation programs in penal institutions, imprisonment does not control a person. It may improve the control system by removing him from society and by serving as a warning to others who might deviate. Even torture, in so far as it is not used to affect other people, involves creation of physical and psychological pain in order to induce a response. Coercion, then, is primarily a method that induces fear of future happenings.

This is just another way of reemphasizing the view of coercion as a method of control that plays on the way a respondent views the future. For control purposes there is no difference between physical coercion and any other kind. However, one of the conditions necessary for radical modifications involves physical dominance, and some states of future physical being appear more real and certain. It is when we examine the limits of coercion as a method of control that we see clearly the importance of recognizing the psychic aspect of all control methods.

The object of this inquiry is the kind of control that is intended to extend over a more remote environment, and our interest in coercion as a method lies in this context. It has been argued that coercion depends for its effectiveness on first inducing discomfort in the respondent, and then inducing the belief that the perceived controller can alleviate the discomfort if the respondent modifies his behavior. As increasing distance comes between controller and respondent many of the characteristics of coercion are changed. The reality, substantiality, and certainty of severe painfulness threatened are reduced for the respondent as space, time, and function (direction and clarity of ongoing relations) intervene between controller and respondent.

It also appears that the individual psyche can rather readily adjust to a perceived potential danger that is constant over time. It seems probable, for example, that no person would support and participate in war if he vividly anticipated as happening to himself what he objectively knows as the worst that can happen to anyone so engaged. But war is big and complex, and battlefields are far away. For the most part a long time elapses between the time a soldier gets into uniform and the time he engages in hand-to-hand combat. The way to battle is slow: he grows accustomed to increasing danger as he takes each step.

Even where severe penalties for crime are certain the rate of crime is greater than one might expect if the severity of the penalty were simply weighed against the benefits of the crime.

Thus even when dire pain is threatened laws are always being violated.

What has been said seems to indicate that maintaining control of a unit of the more remote environment cannot be accomplished by the use of the coercive control method alone. Yet the importance of coercion as a general method is such that all people contribute to a system designed to limit and confine its uses. This arises because of the dangers to general social order that are inherent in it.

The dangers of coercion in any control scheme or system are great and grow out of the nature of the method. The method is most effective under ideal conditions. This creates a strong temptation to use coercion when one wants certain behavior from others and meets heavy resistance. But the ideal conditions include limiting the respondent's choices to several possibilities, all excruciatingly uncomfortable. The more painful it is for a person to engage in the prescribed action in order to alleviate another highly painful condition, the more he will be inclined to do anything to avoid the choice. In short, he will try to increase his alternatives to reduce discomfort and he will come to think that any course of action is preferable to those between which he is forced to choose. As this happens the rationality of his acts will diminish and he will strike out in all directions, disrupting any control scheme. Unsuccessful attempts to use coercion tend to produce less rather than more control, and the disruption may well be in unpredictable places —that is to say, they produce random, not systematic and predictable, behavior. The use of coercion by a controller tends to result in unpredictable coercion and social chaos. Thus with the strong temptation to use coercion because of its immediate effectiveness but with the great danger that once in use there is no way of preventing unwanted consequences, we have a suggestion of why every control system must develop some method for regulating the use of coercion for control of both the immediate and the more remote environment. This brings us to a consideration of the uses of coercion by and in polities.

In most polities there are two general uses of coercion in the system: one confines and limits the general use of coercion, and the second eliminates deviation in specific control schemes, including common positive undertakings. Waging war against another polity is a special case of the use of coercion. The general way coercion is used to control coercion in a polity or control system is for the controllers to designate types of prohibited coercive acts, to threaten countercoercion for violation, and to impose the threatened penalties for actual violation. Permissible coercions are those not specified. For example, in most polities parents are allowed some use of coercion for controlling their children. The permitted varies with culture. The severity of penalties for use of forbidden coercion also varies but not as widely as might be expected, probably because of the recognized danger of coercion.

Much of the danger of coercion as a control method arises from the almost limitless capacity of any one person to induce discomfort in another but the more limited capacity to get a controlled response. Not all induced discomfort is used for control purposes. When this is the case the evoked response may be unpredictable and against control. Thus, in any polity there is a class of proscribed behavior controlled by coercion, precisely because it is a control system and receives its basic support on that basis. Severe discomfort is threatened unless specific behavior is foregone, or performed, depending upon whether a positive or negative command is involved.

The exercise of control not only involves the coercive prohibition of certain acts, but also the prescribing of certain acts that must be performed. Coercion may be used to insure such performance by threatening credibly severe discomforts. The manner in which the payment of some taxes is secured is an example. A taxpayer is told by the controllers that if he refuses to pay a certain amount of money he will be jailed. Alleviation of the discomfort brought on by the prospect of jailing must be weighed against the discomfort of loss of money. There are no other alternatives open to the taxpayer if the control method is effectively used.

No one supposes for a minute that coercion as a control method can account for all taxpaying. It is only one method of control and its main use is to reduce deviation from what can be secured by the other methods of control or from what is habitual. Through socialization, natural disposition, and anticipation of less discomforting consequences most people do not use coercion against others, and do pay their taxes for general polity undertakings. There are always nonconformists: some people use blackmail, some steal, some refuse to pay taxes.

Coercion is used in two ways. One is to force compliance from those who could not be expected to comply until the discomfort is almost a reality. Thus a man is jailed to prevent him from using coercion. He is isolated or quarantined and while he is in jail the unwarranted use of coercion in society is reduced presumably by the amount that he could be expected to produce were he not held in confinement. Beyond this he represents consequences of noncompliance, making the nature of the threatened discomfort more vivid to other persons. It is believed, though not proven, that object lessons of this kind substantially reduce the deviance expected otherwise. We are reminded again of the basic problem of inducing sufficiently severe discomfort to make coercion effective in controlling the more remote environment. The logic of coercion as a control method is such that threatened discomforts are usually made actual acts by inflicting pain mostly to control the behavior of third parties, and hence to maintain the system and to strengthen the predispositions upon which it rests. Putting the recalcitrant taxpayer in jail may or may not get the tax money from him. Executing the murderer neither expunges the wrong he did, nor modifies in any meaningful way the subject's future behavior. Carrying through the threat does affect the anticipated behavior of others and helps account for their compliance and acceptance of control.

A word needs to be said about war as coercion. What we call war may be defined as any effort that involves many people controlling many others predominantly through the use of coercion. Thus we have civil wars and international or inter-polity wars. In a general sense, nothing is more impossible than for many persons to control many others unless there is an extraordinarily effective control structure on each side. War is a highly specialized type of coercion that is designed to control by creating disorganization or inducing a belief that disorganization is imminent. It is not accidental that the word "strategy" finds its main use in war. War clearly shows how all coercion tends to be used strategically, that is, to produce consequences that engender other consequences, and so on to the ultimate point where desired behavior is achieved. War induces discomfort and is designed to weaken the will to resist by committing certain acts in certain places. These acts are undertaken to create the maximum discomfort in those who are not directly and immediately involved. Thus develop notions of strategic military objectives which if reduced will have reverberating consequences. War is a very clear instance of inducing extremely strong discomforts in some in order to have some discomforting effect on many others. Thus there is no war without so-called war atrocities.

The nature of war is such that its widespread use of coercion is extraordinarily difficult to control. It is so disruptive of ongoing control systems that the restoration of order is always a problem. This is why even victors usually do not achieve their control objectives. Unlimited warfare is designed to produce unlimited chaos and the resulting chaos calls for more coercion which in turn produces more chaos.

If coercion is as dangerous and as limited as has been suggested we would expect that well-developed control schemes would have created certain safeguards against its undesirable consequences. In so far as there are rules of warfare, they are designed to reduce adverse consequences from the perspective of control. Within a polity there tends to develop a whole process to determine the limits of the use of coercion and to safeguard its application. Much of this is expressed in the phrase "No person shall deprive any person of life, liberty, or property without due process of law." This means that people can be so deprived with due process of law, and this due process of law is usually widely accepted as the legitimator of the use of coercion. Every polity has something akin to due process of law, and this will be dealt with more explicitly in the chapter on law as an instrument of control. At this point we need only note that there are always efforts to secure the control of the undesired consequences of coercion as a control method.

The use of the coercion method is greatly affected by the intervention of distance between controller and respondent. There is a strong tendency for prospective respondents to discount the probability of threatened injury as more distance comes between them and the controller. The rather drastic effect that distance has on the effectiveness of coercion for control accounts for the extraordinary steps taken to make vivid the severe nature of the threat designed to produce the maximum discomfort. This in turn accounts for the fact that in problems using coercion to control a more remote environment, extreme discomfort is induced in certain individuals, not so much to modify their behavior as to have a discomforting effect on others. In many cultures coercion as a control method raises a profound moral question simply because most coercion in politics is a matter of using some persons as means of controlling other persons.

Because it induces severe discomfort, coercion has a disorganizing effect on the psyche and on interpersonal relations. In order to limit the dangerous consequences and to resolve the moral dilemma posed by coercion, various safeguards are developed. The most important of these safeguards is the provision of an elaborate scheme which selects those to receive the severest discomfort. An example is that of subjecting to the severest discomfort only those who have committed or who have failed to commit certain acts—in short to select them according to due process of law.

Thus we see that coercion is a universal method of exercising control, that it is highly effective in certain limited types of situation, and that its dangers are such as to account for universal methods of safeguarding polities from its chaos-producing potential.

5

Persuasion

It is certainly clear that not all responsive action is brought about by coercion or by proof. In some situations people appear to act in an orderly fashion, pursuant to cues from other persons, yet not as mere extensions of the other persons and not based on an ordered presentation of relevant empirical data. In short, people appear at times to act on uncertain knowledge and yet not under duress imposed by others. We often say of a person in such situations that he "goes along" rather than he "is made" to do this or that. We call this method of control *persuasion*.

What impels people to act at all in response to others when they do not *have* to act? When they do act in apparent response to others, what imparts any pattern to their acts?

We have already developed the hypothesis that people sometimes act when they are subjected to intense discomfort, and that their responsive acts are shaped by the few alternatives permitted them to alleviate discomfort. The pattern imposed by the will of the controller corresponds with the drastic reduction of the free choice of the respondent. In developing this hypothesis we concluded that the main source of intense discomfort is potential injury to self and to objects directly essential to the maintenance of ego-integrity, with the condition that the injury is perceived as substantial and certain. We further concluded that control pattern is affected by the imposition of limited and direct choice.

We are now led to suggest that there is a method of control that induces less severe discomforts and a less narrow and less rigidly imposed set of responses for reducing the discomforts. This is the essence of the method we call persuasion. It is a deliberate control method based upon the exploitation of milder discomforts arising when an object an individual cares about is threatened. As used here objects include, in addition to other persons and tangible objects, beliefs, opinions, myths, ideals, and ideologies. Patterned responsive acts are secured by the controller showing what behavior will alleviate the induced milder discomfort.

A couple of examples will help to make clear the basic process of persuasion as that term is used here. As our first illustration, let us take the case of a controller who wants to convince an individual to buy an automobile from him. The buyer or respondent in this situation can readily check if the car will run, how much gasoline it uses, and how fast it will go. Because he knows the standards of measurement he can judge directly the relative merits of the product, and no other considerations will ordinarily intervene to modify his findings. But suppose that the seller (controller) ascertains that the prospective buyer, whose behavior he is trying to control, has a neighbor he especially likes and respects (for whom he has distinctive feelings of affection and deference), and the seller emphasizes that the neighbor always buys this kind of automobile. If we may assume that all of the direct tests revealed no differences between makes of automobiles, and the buyer purchased an automobile identical to his neighbor's, we would say he was persuaded in so far as his feeling for his neighbor was an element in the transaction. In this case it did not matter whether the moving consideration was his liking for the neighbor or his confidence in the neighbor's judgment. With everything else equal, the buyer chose to bring his action into congruence with that of the neighbor.

How can the roots of this behavior be explained? Obviously the seller had to know the nature of the buyer's feeling for his neighbor, a feeling that could be based upon many things such as appearance, performance, kindness, experience. In any event, the feeling must have been such that once the consideration of the neighbor's automobile was introduced into the situation the buyer felt discomfort at the prospect of being out of harmony with the neighbor. We may say that the seller deliberately created a discomfort and exploited it, because after having aroused the feelings he was in a position to provide alleviation and restoration.

Persuasion as a means of control always involves the introduction of a consideration not naturally relevant to the situation but deliberately made relevant. The persuader must deliberately create and alleviate discomforts in order to control behavior. The essential difference between coercer and persuader is that the former can create severe discomforts in order to modify behavior to his liking, while the latter can only create less severe, or milder discomforts in order to secure complying behavior. There are, of course, important differences in the by-products or unintended consequences. By its nature persuasion is limited to securing marginal and less radical modifications of behavior.

The automobile example involves control in the close-at-hand and intimate environment. What happens when the controller uses persuasion to control on a larger scale? How does one persuade many persons who are scattered over a large area and are not otherwise closely related to each other or to the controller? For example, why does a person vote in an election and why do his choices reveal some pattern, both in his own behavior and between his behavior and that of others. What kind of appeal is made to him by the various would-be controllers who want from him a particular course of action? Under what circumstances can we say that some of his action is due to control?

In general it is easier for a person not to vote than to vote. He has to expend physical energy to get to the polling place, and psychic energy to make his voting choice. The candidate (a representative controller) operates on the assumption that those most likely to vote have some attachment that can be used to induce discomfort. It is usually assumed that the potential voter has an attachment to a previously acquired idea of the good citizen's involvement in community affairs, or that the polity he has previously come to affect requires his help. Contemplating his ideal and his polity as affected objects he is discomforted by the prospect of injury to them caused by his failure to vote. To escape this discomfort he goes to the polls even if no one demonstrates beyond reasonable doubt that a specific desirable consequence will follow from his voting.

But merely voting, going to the polls, produces few meaningful consequences unless there is some pattern to the choice made. Each voter might end up voting for himself and produce chaos instead of control. Therefore the various controllers must impose some pattern on the choice that is made. In order to get the voter to choose A rather than B he must be provided with a basis for choosing A. The controller candidate again takes what he supposes to be the objects of the voters' attachments and tries to induce discomfort by showing that objects he affected would be better off by an A vote and that those which repelled him would be worse off, or that an A vote would be the kind of vote that an affected object would want him to cast. In an actual election the whole gamut of possible objects of attachment and repulsion are exploited in this fashion. They include love of motherhood, love of God, country, party, causes, ideals (such as democracy), and so on. The controller tries to find the stronger attachments and then show how a vote for him would preserve and enhance the object of the attachment. What the voter responds to favorably will be a synthesis of his own attachments and his ordering of them as this ordering is influenced by the controller.

Before going on it may be helpful to explain why the word persuasion has been chosen for this method of control. Other words or phrases that might have been used to characterize the method of control that we are here concerned with are *influence, authority,* or *manipulation of incentives.* The word "influence," which is widely used in discussing politics, was rejected because it tends through usage to cover too much. It suggests effects produced by the stars or other inanimate forces, as well as the effect of one person on another. Even in modern usage it emphasizes a complex of forces operating in a rather mysterious fashion. Persuade, however, emphasizes deliberate or calculated control acts of human beings, and thus is much more specific for our present purposes. Influence may be thought of as being used in persuasion.

Authority is an unsatisfactory term because the only verb form of the word, authorize, begs the central question, and control methods must be described by verbs, preferably strong verbs that emphasize cause and effect and not states of being. The word "authority" stresses the author of a control act, but knowing the author tells us nothing about why a particular act has certain consequences. Although control cannot be explained by authority, control theory must be broad enough to explain the function of author or authority in control. Authority is a conferred right to act and generally speaking it makes a difference in the response to a person's control act if he is regarded as having or not having a right to act. Authority and right refer to qualities in control acts but are not control acts. Authority suggests a static quality of patterns in human relations, whereas persuade suggests reciprocation and action.

Manipulation of incentives suggests a control method similar to the one we call persuasion. An incentive incites action by arousing feelings of attraction or repulsion for the phenomenon the controller introduces into a situation and which he may use manipulatively to modify the behavior of the respondent. Inducement to action by incentive also suggests that an individual's desire for one thing is used to get him to perform some other unrelated act. When a man works for money we say money is an incentive to work. However, the advantage that the word "persuade" has over the phrase "manipulation of incentives" is that it refers more precisely and economically to a range of control acts that we want to explore. Incentives are used in persuading, but also used are other entities of attraction or repulsion not ordinarily called incentives.

What we try to account for by using the verb "persuade" and the noun "persuasion" are instances in which one person gets another person to do something by appealing to his milder likes and dislikes and to his less firmly and clearly held cognitions. As Rousseau suggests, we are concerned with those things a person does because he is persuaded without being convinced. One is convinced, in the sense used here, when he arrives at a course of action by direct and independent examination of the consequences of alternative courses of action. Persuasion suggests acting on faith, belief, feelings, hunch, unconsciousness and uncertainty. The psychological bases of persuasion are likes and dislikes, attractions and repulsions, comforts and discomforts, beliefs and rejections, the familiar and the unfamiliar, and the customary and the innovative.

The method of control we call persuasion is, like coercion, made up of two steps. The first is to arouse discomfort with a state of nonaction, and the second is to limit the action alternatives and thus impose a pattern on them. The difference, of course, is that coercion arouses action by threatening those very high values which verge over to perceived necessity, and then makes alleviation of the discomfort by action contingent upon narrowly prescribed responsive acts. These narrowly prescribed responsive acts can approach but not equal the discomfort wrought in the first instance. Thus we say that radical changes in otherwise expected behavior always suggests but do not prove the use of coercion.

A great many objects of attachment can be utilized by the method of persuasion. Nevertheless they do reflect some order both within an individual and between some or all individuals. As we have argued above, all individuals have an attachment to a particular polity—to tribe, community, customs, ceremonies, class, myths, race, and so on. There may also be a wide variety of persons, heroes, idols, villains, and a wide variety of inanimate objects including symbolic representations like flag, mace, scepter, and the like. Any object that is cognized probably is evaluated, thus creating a feeling of attraction or repulsion. Even though many of these orientations are latent most of the time, they still create predispositions to act in certain ways and are capable of arousing and shaping action. The basis of attachment to these objects is a mixture of the ethical, aesthetic, and metaphysical, but the important thing is that each in some degree is viewed not as simple and direct means, but also as an end in itself.

Before passing on to a more direct consideration of persuasion in politics, we should note in general terms the inherent limits on the method of persuasion. In the first place, the controller for the most part works with the attachments that the respondent already has. The essential nature of attachments is such that all but the most ephemeral are acquired slowly, mainly through the socialization process. This limits what the controller can appeal to and to whom he can appeal, for both the attachments and their ranking varies widely with culture and even within a culture between persons of different backgrounds and experiences. A particular object may evoke a positive attractiveness for one person but be anathema to another. This makes a special limitation on persuading many persons to the same course of action.

Another limitation arises out of the factor of credibility. It should be clear that what has been called attachment to objects consists of a more rational relation than one which might evoke mere ejaculation. Because this attachment is rather a mixture of rational and irrational, the respondent may be expected to have some sense of the appropriateness of the course of action prescribed by the controller. One of the practical risks that a controller runs in using persuasion is that of overestimating the respondent's gullibility, thereby damaging his own cause. There are limits beyond which people cannot be fooled, and the controller must work within these limits.

Another limitation arises out of the fact that the controller finds it difficult to foreclose other courses of action pursuant to the discomfort he initially arouses. By proceeding indirectly through his attachments to shape the behavior of the respondent, he cannot avoid creating opportunities for alternative courses of action, which implies that there is a certain danger in arousing the discomfort. To arouse a person to vote may cause him to cast a vote that is against the wishes of the person who aroused him in the first place.

Finally, because the respondent is conscious of the controller or the control agency or agent, the controller must limit his behavior so that it does not discredit his other manipulations.

All of these limitations grow out of the nature of the method. They also suggest the limits of effectiveness of the method from the respondent's point of view. He can procrastinate, avoid, rationalize, discuss, check, and so on. Thus, when time is of the essence or when precise responses are needed by the controller, persuasion is obviously a limited method.

Persuasion, like coercion, is a general method of deliberate or calculated control. It is used for immediate and intermediate ends, and to control others who are already closely related and close in space. What happens when distance intervenes between the controller and his objective and the respondent and his response? What happens when strangers try to control strangers who are far away in time, space, and day-to-day relations? And what happens when the control effort is designed to secure interlocking behavior on the part of great numbers and diversities of ongoing relations? These are the control problems that produce politics and bring into play the method of persuasion.

The distinctiveness of politics arises out of the character of the controllers, the objects of attachment they exploit, and the end for which control is sought. One of the critical problems in persuasion is for the controller to get anyone to pay attention to his message. The problem becomes greater as more distance intervenes. The more people to whom the controller addresses his appeal, the greater the proportion who are either unconscious of his existence or who, in the universal competition for attention, do not give him access in the first instance. Under these conditions we would expect the controller of a more remote environment to develop techniques and practices to get himself known and positively affected. One would also expect that those interested in the development and maintenance of a control system under these conditions would develop practices enabling greater accessibility. The greater reliance placed on persuasion, the greater the importance of the practice. One person can make an appeal on the radio or in the newspapers and virtually no one will get his message. Another person, seemingly similar in age, sex, wisdom, and the like, may deliver the same appeal to millions of rapt readers or listeners. The simple fact that the latter person is the President of the United States may not be directly revealed by looks or behavior. We can only conclude that he receives the differential response because he is perceived as a special kind of object by many persons. Thus are offices created and attachments to them acquired and made ready for exploitation.

In the face of remoteness the effectiveness of persuasion for control requires limited and differentiated controllers. These are limited and differentiated by the respondent so he can sort out the messages. We should conclude from this that in cases where persuasion is effective in ordering control the persuaders or controllers are limited, well known, and ordinarily deferred to. We should also expect to see a structure of offices to enhance the personality of a few. In situations of less remoteness we should expect to see less emphasis on this magnification and depersonalization of the controller. This produces the familiar political situation in which the speaker's status is more important than what he says or asks. Distance also makes a difference in the objects of attachment that can be expected to arouse people, and the character of these objects is important in shaping the control system as well as in securing specific kinds of behavior.

The most distinctive and universal attachment is the polity. This object or entity incorporates the greatest diversity and comprehensiveness that is perceived as a unit. Beyond this boundary are others who perceive it as an object and who may have a range of feelings toward it, but who do not have a feeling of mutual possession. Exploiting attachments to this type of object is the basic process of political persuasion, and since persuasion plays the dominant role in controlling within this object it may be regarded practically as the basic political process. Political control is distinguished from all other control by virtue of its appeal to do things for love of country, an appeal presented in many different ways but which adds up to the same thing.

Securing behavior necessary for systematic control in a more remote environment is never easy and in many ways is not even natural. What happens to strangers far away or in the future is always being crowded by nearer and more pressing concerns. Yet there is a universal but vague sense that things out of sight may somehow be important. For control purposes this vague sense must be converted into specific acts and restraints; it must have limits that are sufficiently extended to provide objective strength and assurance and sufficiently limited to constitute, both in perception and in objective fact, a viable and distinctive object or entity. Thus we would expect that the more distance that intervenes between controllers and controlled, the more prominent would be the attachment to polity in the process of control in general and of control by persuasion in particular.

Most of the objects of attachment which are exploited in the process of controlling the more remote environment are related to polity. This is true of ideology, ideals, groups, public leaders, works of art, and in fact countless other objects of attachment. Even coercion is almost useless for control unless it is legitimated and legitimation is essentially a process of persuasion based on previously acquired attachments that tend to be related to polity.

Because they embrace such great diversity, polity undertakings necessarily require widely shared interlocking behavior, either to undertake a program of positive action or to inhibit certain kinds of deviance. Thus one would expect to find political controllers seeking reenforcement and support for the polity-relevant course of action they prescribe and to do this by appealing to other attachments for that purpose. In turn this would lead to the more extensive use of widely shared attachments that are more clearly related to the polity. The common objects used in the United States are trade unions, business enterprises, and ethnic groupings. These attachments will be explored in greater detail in the last part of this book.

If the problem of controlling through persuasion in the more remote environment is distinctive by virtue of the controllers and the objects of attachment exploited, we should also expect the ends of control action to be distinctive. And this is clearly the case. One of the main reasons to support control within a unit of more remote environment is to assure a certain orderliness with the security that it provides. A polity is always a unit that reflects and maintains security for those who cleave to it. Thus the appeal to maintain order in the polity is a strong one, and a viable polity is vigorously supported by most people. Moreover, people are readily persuaded to courses of action which are shown to provide this security. In forging the patterns of response to control necessary for maintaining order and security, people gradually develop a *system* of control and this system, reflecting as it does reasonably stable interaction patterns, can be used for a wide variety of large-scale, cooperative undertakings less and less directly related to the problem of insuring general orderliness and common defense. Once a people has been convinced to pay high taxes for defense they can be induced to pay taxes for schools, recreation, conservation of resources, and for many other purposes.

Thus the ends for which persuasion can be used in the polity come increasingly to encompass life's activities, as long as their support is based on the welfare of the polity.

The difference between coercion and persuasion lies not in the fundamental nature of the control process, but in the respondent's perception of and relation to objects. Whereas coercion exploits those objects the respondent perceives as directly and immediately necessary to his existence, persuasion exploits those objects which are of more remote concern. Thus persuasion is the main method through which the more remote environment is controlled, and control of the more remote environment is limited to the extent that the persuasional method of control is limited.

Since persuasion is the dominant political method and since the polity is the main object orientation exploited for control purposes, the question arises as to the possibilities of rational or certain political knowledge. If people are asked to give compliance and support on the basis of what is good and bad for the polity, is it possible for political action to relate ends and means effectively? A polity, either as it is perceived or as it exists as an independent object, is such a large and complex object that it seems impossible to determine with any certainty whether the discrete act of a discrete person is good or bad for it. When equally wise men urge diametrically opposed courses of action, both arguing that unless his prescription is followed the polity will disintegrate, whom is the potential respondent supposed to follow, or how is he to arrive at his own conclusion? It is this question that reminds us of the enduring irrational element in all politics, irrational here simply meaning action undertaken without an obvious relation between means and ends. The method of persuasion is used where such elements of irrationality are present. Persuasion ceases to be persuasion when it does not utilize faith, confidence, myth, belief, opinion, love, loyalty, allegiance, beauty, respect, authority, and other factors that imply feeling rather than knowledge.

But persuasion in politics also has its rational side. There are two reasons for this. In the first place, it seems unlikely that a person perceives and orients to any object without some understanding of it. There is always the cognitive element in orientation, which carries with it a highly certain knowledge of ends and means. The only objects about which an individual has absolutely no solidly based knowledge are those which he does not perceive. This is a psychological hypothesis but it seems a plausible and a necessary one if we are not to write off the political enterprise as hopeless. In the second place, there is accumulated through trial-and-error experience particles of certain knowledge of what is involved in controlling the more remote environment, and hence what is good and bad for the polity as an object. These particles of certain knowledge penetrate the enduring objects of faith, confidence, and myth, and are carried embedded in them down through time. It is suggested that the objects of faith would not be carried down through time unless such particles were embedded in them. Thus we are led to conclude that in exploiting attachments or orientations to objects there are always elements of both the rational and irrational fused together.

6

Proof

It has been our contention here that the basic way one person exercises control over another is to induce discomfort in the respondent and then make alleviation contingent upon a behavioral modification. The problem of the controller is to induce the discomfort and gain acceptance of the course of action that will effect his control objective. This process implies that the steady state of being of the respondent is one of inertia or resistance to deliberately induced change. This is emphasized because in order to observe the process of control we must focus upon those instances in which we believe that the respondent would not behave the way he does pursuant to the intended control act. When we have reason to believe that one actor will behave in the way prescribed by another actor without the intervention of an intended control act, it is impossible to attribute the action to the intervention of a controller.

We have developed two methods of control, distinguished by the severity of the discomfort and the narrowness of the alleviating responses from which the respondent may choose. The more radical the modification, the greater the induced discomfort and the narrower and more inescapable the choice—hence the more coercive the method. However, as one moves across the scale of discomfort and of increased alternatives, the control method becomes more and more persuasive. Although one method passes over to the other gradually at the ends of the scale, there is a clear distinction between the two methods.

This brings us to the consideration of a third basic method of control, which we call proof. We suggest that the effectiveness of proof as a control method relies upon the exploitation of still milder discomforts and a greater self-chosen course of action.

It should be emphasized at the outset that what we are interested in here is not primarily how something is proven, but how the method of proof is used in exercising control over people. It seems likely that every people or culture has a stock of certain knowledge. Furthermore, it seems likely that in every culture there is some widely accepted method for gaining and disseminating certain knowledge. Subsequent changes may challenge or disprove this knowledge and the processes for finding it may become unreliable. For purposes of men controlling other men, the belief that some things are certain is more important than actual certainty.

Proof as a control method first induces discomfort in the respondent by attacking either his existing certain knowledge or his less-than-certain knowledge, or by proposing that certain knowledge can be substituted for his uncertain knowledge. In contemporary Western culture the most accepted method for ascertaining certain knowledge is proof or scientific proof. In discussing the methods of coercion and persuasion we spoke of exploiting the respondent's orientations or attachments to perceived objects in his environment. Rather than exploiting objects, even as they were broadly defined, proof exploits an orientation to a state of mind regarding certainty. It exploits a yearning for certain knowledge.

When an individual becomes certain in knowledge in an area in which he was previously uncertain, or when doubt is cast on the truth of what he thought was certain knowledge, he is stirred to seek fuller knowledge and use it as a basis for his action. The distinguishing characteristic of proof as a method is that it provides a basis for the individual to arrive at his own alternative course of action. Even though it offers few choices, control through proof does approach self-control, at least for those who are capable of applying the process of proof to a problem. For the person who cannot apply the process of proof himself the control method is a variation of the method of persuasion.

Before proceeding further it may help in understanding control through proof to point out that there is a culture-bound aspect to what we call scientific proof. We have already suggested that every culture has its method for establishing certain knowledge. Thus, perceiving any knowledge as certain is more a matter of prior confidence in the method or process than it is actual certainty of knowledge. It is faith in the process that produces and validates the sense of certainty. Thus any process that establishes a sense of certainty may be said to produce and validate certain knowledge. For control purposes it would have the same effect as scientific proof or any other accepted method. The superiority of scientific proof rests on its open-mindedness, which insists upon constantly validating the process by comparing it with its consequences. In this way the findings are kept close to what all people can check by sense impression. Nevertheless it does need to be emphasized that even scientific proof when used for control depends upon confidence in the method.

The nature of proof as a method of control may be clarified by the following simple illustrations. We expect that an individual engaged in manufacturing steel shafts will continue using the same alloy, unless, for example, someone comes up with a proposal for a variation in the alloy. On the basis of this proposal a shaft is made with the new alloy which tests prove to be stronger. As a result of these tests the shaft-maker alters his alloy in order to change the shafts. Here we would be justified in saying that the individual changed his behavior because it was proved empirically the change would improve his product. It was discomforting for him to contemplate the old way in the light of the certain knowledge he had acquired about the new method.

As a second illustration, let us take an individual who plans a trip and who marks out his intended route (which becomes his ordinarily expected course of travel, his behavior). However, a friend takes the map and shows him a shorter route, which the traveler then follows. This would be a case of empirical proof if the traveler actually traversed both routes and determined that the second one was in fact shorter. Otherwise the proof would be persuasional, based upon his willingness to trust a map and the map-maker. A similar case is that of a traveler who when reminded that a straight line is the shortest path between two points modifies his plans accordingly and shortens his route.

Another example is that of a merchant who has never handled a particular line of goods and who does not expect to change. One day, however, a salesman for that line tells him that other merchants who have handled his goods have increased their profits. The merchant checks the records of the other merchants, ascertains that the only difference between his situation and theirs is that he does not handle the particular line, and on the basis of this finding modifies his behavior and stocks the new line.

These are all very simple examples of how proof is used to control behavior. The controller is in all cases the individual who introduces change into the situation with the intention of getting another individual (respondent) to make specific modifications in his behavior. By examining our examples in greater detail we can get a better idea of what the process of proof involves and what are the conditions essential to its effective use as a means of control. In the first place, the examples lead us to distinguish between logical deductive proof and empirical or inductive proof. The traveler who took the straight-line route made his choice on the basis of a few self-evident truths and a few plausible conventions of the process of proof. The man who changed his alloy probably insisted that enough tests be run showing the alloy to be capable of maintaining its superiority under all probable conditions. Hence we say he relied upon empirical proof.

What these examples of proof as a means of modifying behavior have in common is that the consequences of the introduction of a change in a situation can be accurately predicted and communicated. Basically, of course, men are moved to change because they have confidence that pursuant to proof one known change will take place when one known but different change is introduced. Since it is confidence that underlies the stimulus to change, proof is akin to persuasion; the two differ mainly in the level and basis of the confidence. People only respond to proof if they are prepared to do so; that is to say, if they are conditioned to respond to it. Unlike response to coercion, response to proof does not come naturally; it has to be acquired.

What do our simple examples indicate about the conditions necessary in Western culture for the operation of proof as a means of control? First, the objective must be simple, clear, and determinate. In the case of the shaft-maker it was a matter of strength of the shaft. Behind this there was probably the consideration of increased sales and profits. In the case of the travelers, proof was based on a single consideration of distance. Conventions about measuring linear distance are agreed to widely and generally, but if considerations of road conditions, safety, scenic qualities, and so on were introduced, the whole scheme of proof would have to be changed. In the case of the merchant, it was assumed that increased sales was the objective agreed upon by the controller and the controlled. All of this would suggest that the use of proof as a means of control is limited to those situations where a simple and determinate objective is understood by both controller and controlled.

Since proof depends on the prior existence of a sense of certainty that a changed act will lead to a known change in consequence, it must be possible to predict cause and effect accurately at each step in the chain of proof. Unless this is so there cannot be a basis for full confidence in the prediction of the objective or end result. Moreover, proof has either to ignore by-product consequences or be able to predict all of them. Otherwise the course of action that proof seems to dictate may be too costly for adoption. This is another way of saying that in proof it is impossible to handle a large number of variables. Either there has to be only a limited number of variables or many of them must be disregarded in order to make the proof manageable. The mere passage of time introduces into all proof a variable that can create doubt, unless time change can be compensated for or conclusively shown to be irrelevant.

When proof is used as a means of control by humans over humans there is a severe limitation on experimentation, the very foundation of empirical proof. For example, it is not practical to experiment with selective breeding in order to find out what makes good citizens. All that can be done is to observe what happens and try to find causal patterns. This makes the problem of controlling the variables highly complicated. Uncontrolled variables enter into the situation and must be taken into account in making inferences, whereas in an experiment variables are deliberately manipulated and stabilized. This is not to say that proof is impossible, or that experiments are not possible as a means of proving. It does mean that proof is effective as a means of control only under limited conditions.

Up to now we have been talking about proof in general, regardless of what is being proved and to whom. Now we turn to a consideration of proof as it operates in controlling relations among humans and more particularly as it operates in exercising control over large numbers of diverse persons in a variety of situations.

There is the problem of the use of proof when an attempt is made to control the behavior of several persons simultaneously. By its nature proof is more effective when one person proves to another the best possible course of action among the available alternatives. This is because it is easier for two individuals than for many to agree upon a specific objective. As a general proposition the more persons there are the simpler the change must be.

It is also important to note that it is one thing to get verbal acceptance of a proof, but quite another matter to get the indicated action. Take for example the use of polio vaccine. Given the evidence of the vaccine's effect on the disease, it is surprising that so many persons are still unvaccinated. Even though it can safely be assumed that most people in the United States do not want to be victims of polio, many do not respond to proof as a means of control. The only plausible explanation is that they do not all perceive the danger to themselves in the same degree, and perhaps even in the same way. Or perhaps we may say this is a case of a difference between belief and action. Action does not always follow belief. If asked, most persons probably would say they believed that the vaccine sharply reduces the chances of being infected with polio virus, but some fail to act personally on this belief. On the other hand, the effectiveness of proof may be limited even when a single controller and controlled are interacting. This is because cause and effect are so complicated that any possible proof leaves room for substantial doubt. We may summarize by saying that even in simple matters the effectiveness of proof is more limited as the number of individuals increases. Then as the matter of proof becomes less simple the limits of proof narrow even when the number of persons remains constant.

This brings us to the use of proof as a means of control in politics and the more remote environment. As a common practice proof in politics is used most often and most rigorously in controlling the behavior of persons who themselves use the means of coercion for controlling behavior. In a polity where the differentiated scheme of control is well developed, proof finds its main use in controlling the choices of judges or juries who themselves use the method of coercion or do not intervene to control behavior with coercion, beyond, of course, the requirements for submitting to the process of proof. Evidence seems to indicate a certain universality in the practice of using a well-defined and accepted process of reaching a decision to inflict coercion. Even trial by ordeal was based upon the form of proof: withstanding the ordeal was proof of innocence.

It is interesting to examine the reasons for the association of proof and coercion in polity control systems. Proof is the most certain basis of action, but its very certainty grows out of the narrow situations to which it is applicable. Moreover, its effectiveness depends upon a strong commitment to the process itself, even when the findings run against the feelings. Coercion, as has been shown, is not only based on the most severe type of discomfort that man can inflict on man but it is also potentially the most dangerous and disruptive, capable at any time of producing chaos unless the use of coercion itself as a means of control is carefully controlled and used for severely limited and carefully defined purposes. The existence of a court system represents an attempt to limit the users of coercive control. The requirement that the few who apply coercion apply it only pursuant to proof and that coercion be used for specific, agreed-upon ends indicates recognition of the restricted conditions under which proof is useful. One can also, of course, associate the use of proof with a moral theory based upon respect for the autonomy of the individual personality, and thus the case for its increased use can be strengthened. But the point to be emphasized here is that its use is necessary if the ends of control itself are not to be negated by the uncontrolled and imprecise use of coercion.

In the final analysis proof depends for its precision and strategic effectiveness upon a widespread commitment to it as a respected process. This is another way of saying that proof is a formal convention. In order to stabilize the process of proof one must be able to check the results independently. The formality of the process of proof in a court of law is again a good example of this. As soon as proof depends upon a particular judge, jury, or process it loses its compelling qualities and makes room for expediency. The more proof depends upon the personality of a clever lawyer, the more the control involved uses the means of persuasion.

Proof is most useful when the ultimate objective of control involves man's relationship with inanimate objects. By using proof an engineer can convince those who are building a bridge that the beams should be stronger. Here proof can provide a basis for modifying the behavior of men, but the final objective is the size of steel beams. Proof is limited as a basis for securing modifications where there is no final reference to measurable qualities. Try to prove, for example, that there should be a year added to or subtracted from the school

Proof   [129]

program. Either would modify human behavior, but which qualities—happiness, adjustment, ability—would be considered, and if they could be agreed upon, how would they be measured? This again emphasizes that the usefulness of proof depends upon agreement about the end. In many matters proof is an invaluable means of modifying and controlling human behavior, but its main value is in the day-to-day administration of affairs, including public affairs. A certain machine will save so much money and time; a certain building will cost so much and provide so much new space. These are essentially simple matters because they involve a narrow range of considerations.

The degree of respect for proof as a basis of action, as well as the methods of proof, will vary among cultures and subcultures. In a culture where respect is high for a particular process of proof one would expect that even when actual proof is impossible the form of proof would be used to control behavior. For example, a great deal of campaign oratory in the United States purports to be proof. The campaigner attempts to elicit certain action from people by "proving" to them that choosing him or a member of his party would produce certain results. He quotes statistics, makes appeals to logic, cites cases, in the hope that respect for the form of proof will lead people to accept his prescriptions without checking his evidence. Proof is widely used in this way in legislative bodies, despite the fact that most matters that come before a legislative body do not lend themselves to proof. What happens is that the form of proof becomes an entity for which feelings of confidence and respect are developed, and these become the basis of persuasion.

Since proof has a very limited effectiveness in getting large numbers of remotely related persons to modify their behavior, we would expect that in intercultural control the process of proof would work only where the certain knowledge is shared by the two cultures. The structure of international relations is such that no objective is simple and, even if it seems to be, the calculation of by-products or unintended consequences is so important and so difficult that proof finds little use.

Considering a control system in a polity as a whole, of course, proof plays an important strategic role, as we shall see when we examine the various instruments of control.

THREE

Instruments
of Control

A controller, whether an individual or group, faces two problems that must be solved simultaneously. The best solution of each always tends to be antagonistic to the best solution of the other. Thus an enduring tension exists in all control systems. One of the problems that always confronts a controller is how to get acceptance of, and compliance with, the behavior he prescribes. We have developed the general methods available to him, but these are not effective for control unless they are appropriately applied. The second problem is to make the right prescription. By right prescription is meant that course of behavior expected to result in the accomplishment of the particular control objective. No intended control can be effective unless these two conditions are met, and there can be no effective control system unless both conditions are effectively met.

The difficulty of the political control system becomes apparent when we contemplate what the factor of distance or remoteness adds to the difficulty of solving each problem. This is to say nothing of reconciling the two, for they must be reconciled if there is to be an appropriate result from intended control acts. As control is extended over an ever more remote environment the securing of responses becomes more difficult because more people and greater diversity are involved. Moreover, the intervention of greater spatial, temporal, and functional distance makes it more difficult to determine what is the appropriate behavior for achieving the control objective.

Given the intrinsic difficulty of these two problems when taken together, one would expect that through a combination of trial, error, and invention specialized devices would be created to aid the controller in meeting these problems. Such devices have indeed come into existence and we shall call them instruments of control. The word instrument is derived from the Latin *instruer,* meaning to construct, furnish, provide, equip, build in or on. It is defined as that by means of which any work is performed or result is effected. Thus, instrument implies a deliberate adding to man's capacity to achieve purposes. We are concerned here primarily, of course, with those instruments which man forges in order to add to his capacity to control his more remote human environment. The basic methods of control that have been suggested and explained have to be used in order to be effective and they cannot be used directly and singly except for the most simple and obvious kind of control. Because man is anxious about his more remote environment and has a will to control it, he creates and supports instruments that enable him to control more effectively that about which he has developed a concern.

An instrument is something that is made, fashioned, or adapted. There are two elements in any instrument: the medium or material and the shaping and adapting contributed by the instrument maker. With this conception of an instrument one would expect to find control instruments reflecting the nature of the particular control problem.

Instruments are developed to secure acceptance of prescriptions by all whose behavior is relevant. Control is so important that no control system can rely entirely upon whim or personality and get maximum acceptance. Therefore a more stable, visible, and elaborate object must be created, and intended respondents must be made conscious of this object. That is to say, they must be brought to perceive it and orient to it in a particular way. Within tolerable limits all persons whose behavior is relevant must orient to it in essentially the same way. This orientation must be such that when a controller speaks through or on behalf of the object it will increase the probability of conformity to what is prescribed. The respondent must become predisposed to follow cues given through the object more regularly and certainly than he would if the controller prescribed directly, in his own name and on his own behalf. In short, the orientation must have the effect of magnifying and enhancing the controller. The contemplation of not following prescriptions through the object must be capable of producing discomfort, which will initiate action toward compliance. This means that the cognitive aspect of an orientation to the instrumental object must contain some understanding of who speaks for the object. It must also include an ability to understand the symbolic representations of such spokesmen, and the legitimating process which specifies the spokesman. Titles, uniforms, elections, appointments, are all used to symbolize and limit spokesmen for the object, and indirectly for the controller. When an individual comes to the door and says that he is Inspector Smith of the FBI, the respondent will react in a certain way, based on his prior orientation to the FBI. This then is the basic way in which object-instruments help to get acceptance for control acts.

The second problem for the controller which requires instruments, is to make a prescription that is appropriate to the control end sought. For this purpose each instrument has a specialized process designed to reduce errors in judgment and to adapt the means to the end in view. Division of labor, specialization, fact gathering, experimenting, and experience are all consequences of efforts by controllers to make appropriate prescriptions. It is expected that the FBI agent will ask questions designed to secure relevant information.

The source of the tension between the two control needs is obvious. Unacceptable responsive action may, in view of the control objective, be the most appropriate action to prescribe. In a party platform, for example, this tension is exaggerated. The party viewed as a vote-getting instrument or object reflects in its platform a balance between appropriate action and acceptable action. If appropriate action seems to call for a tax increase, the prescription will be modified in view of the problem of acceptability. And for an instrument to be effective when control is extended over distance, the general acceptability of the object must be enhanced. For if one prescription reduces respect for or confidence in the instrument as an entity it will tend to be a less effective instrument in other situations.

Three types of instruments have developed to facilitate extending control over a more remote environment by enhancing the effectiveness of controllers. These instruments, which we shall call law, agency, and agent, are interrelated, ordered, and specialized and can be identified in all polities. Each is designed to enhance the conformity to prescribed behavior and to increase the appropriateness of the prescribed behavior. They are differentiated by the degrees of generality and priority of the control they help impose. When there is conflict their prescriptions of behavior are ranked in precedence of obligation.

Law is used to help achieve the most general conformity, and a lawful or legalized prescription has the highest priority. It has more refined processes for helping to increase the probability of rightness or appropriateness of prescriptions made through it or in its name. Law also bears a special relation to the methods of control since it is used to regulate coercion and to regulate and secure compliance in many areas through the use of coercion. Law helps to impose what might be called a first order of control.

Agency is used to help get the next lower level of priority of acceptance and to bring about a more specialized, positive, and detailed compliance with prescribed behavior. Law and agency supplement each other both in the application of control methods and in assuring the appropriateness of prescribed behavior. Law is used either positively or negatively to regulate basic aspects of agency.

Agent is used primarily to get strategic acceptance and conformity in which tension between the best prescription and highest probability of compliance are reconciled in a specific control situation. The agent helps to link the more remote and the close at hand so that the result is a continuous control system. Finally, in situations that are strategic to the control problem, or to the system, the agent brings a combination of all control methods to bear on the solution of the control problem. The prescriptions made through an agent have the lowest priority and least autonomy, and because they are predominantly strategic they are the least general in application but most variable in form and content.

7

Law

Where the existence of political phenomena is indicated by regularity and pattern in human relations encompassing considerable time, space and diverse functions there is a tendency to attribute it to something called law. As a corollary, we say that if one wants to establish regularity and system in interpersonal relations over a considerable span of time, space, and diversity of functions then law must be used to do it. All of this is another way of raising the question of whether law creates regularity and control or whether it reflects them. There has to be a starting place for analysis and we choose to start with the notion of law as an instrument through which man uses the means available to him both to create and to perfect a certain orderliness, regularity, predictability, and achievement of goals in a particular segment of his environment. Since law is regarded as an instrument for present purposes, we must first ascertain some of the implications of an instrumental view of law.

There is everywhere a certain regularity in human relations characterized by degrees of longevity, pervasiveness, inclusiveness, consistency, and purposiveness that we would not expect any individual man to be able to impart intentionally to his relations with his fellow men. But man armed with law, so to speak, seems to modify these regularities in varying degrees. What is man armed with when he is armed with the law?

A man is armed with the law when he effects a modification in the behavior of another person that would not be expected unless he spoke in the name of the law or was thought to speak in the name of the law. Law operates directly as a control instrument when an individual modifies an act to make it conform with what he perceives to be the standards set by law. In other words, law is an instrument of control both when the controlled perceives a spokesman of the law, and when he perceives the rules of law as standard-setting or measuring instruments to guide and limit his acts.

That a judge is an ordinary man armed with the law is obvious. But the notion of man being armed with the instrument of law is more universal and less formalistic. For example, a person starts to pick a flower in a park when a total stranger comes along, a man who is not perceived as an official or lawyer, and says that it is against the law to pick flowers there. The would-be flower picker stops; a new consideration has been brought to his attention. The law has intervened in the situation. One person has modified the behavior of another person, simply by introducing the word symbol "law." It is fairly certain had the stranger said, "Don't pick that flower, I want it," he would not have been successful. Of course he might have been bluffing; there might have been no such law, or he might not have known if there was or not. This only suggests, however, that law is the kind of instrument that affects the psyche, and that what affects the psyche depends as much upon what the psyche is prepared to respond to as it does upon the environmental change. The element of bluff here is no different from what causes a man to turn over his money to someone brandishing a toy pistol. What is important is that the victim perceives the pistol as real.

It is obvious from what has been said that law is useful as an instrument of control only where both the controller and the controlled perceive or have an image of something named law, and that this perception or image generates a certain sensitivity, a sense of obligation, respect, or fear. If a rule modifies behavior because it is simply a good rule that people already agree with, the fact that it is called law makes no difference in the degree of its effectiveness. If one man obeys another because he likes him or fears him, his being a law-sayer neither adds to nor detracts from his effectiveness.

We can best see the effectiveness of law as an instrument of control in cases where people modify their behavior to conform to a rule that they do not like and do not agree with simply because they believe in respecting some entity symbolized by the word "law." If he is amenable to it, an individual can to a degree read the law, as he can read a ruler, and measure and shape his own behavior, or another can introduce considera-tion of the law into a situation and thereby get him to conform his behavior. Thus law as an instrument can be both a measure and a tool.

Because of its nature and the beliefs from which it is fash-ioned, no one person or group of persons can create law. In this sense it comes into existence of its own accord. But this is deceptive. Man creates the instrument of law more or less as a by-product of his will to control and order relations in the world he perceives as relevant to him. Thus any law, in the sense of legal system, reflects much of the purposes of a whole people in a polity and also their notion of the regularity and order that are both functional for, and congenial to, most of them. Law is a genuine social product, a kind of a master instrument. It is an instrument for facilitating the most general control of man over man. In some form or another it is always found where strangers mingle.

Law is always a complicated instrument, and in a polity that is advanced and extensive in space, time, and function it is especially complex. Yet we may say that it is composed of parts that have an organic or mechanical relation to one another. There are four major components of law, and in their perception of the law different persons may be more cognizant of, and responsive to, any one or several of these components. Nevertheless the independent observer may identify all four. They are rules, perception or image, lawmen or lawsayers, and jurisdiction.

A rule is simply a prescribed course of behavior in a specified situation. By itself it is not law, but without rules there is no law. When we say a rule is prescribed we mean that it is announced in advance. Thus it is forward looking or prospective. On the basis of experience and foresight controllers anticipate situations and specify the behavior that is to be expected in such situations. A rule is a rule, regardless of who announces it and regardless of what it deals with, as long as it prescribes a course of conduct in a given situation. In this sense, then, we may say that whether a phenomenon is a rule or not is purely a matter of form. The kind of rules that are a component of law depend upon their operating in an organic or mechanical relation with the other components of law.

The next component of law is a perception or image of an entity called "the law," "the law of the land," or "the legal system." There is no viable law in a particular polity unless there is substantial similarity in the images it evokes for different people. The less similarity, the less effective the instrument, and the greater the similarity, the more effective the instrument. Rules of law, we may now say, are rules which are perceived as being rules of law. If we could measure the difference in effectiveness of any rule and a rule of law we could ascertain and measure the effectiveness of law *qua* law. In the modern world we are aware of the enormous time and energy that go into changing, improving, and adjusting the rules of law. We are less aware of what goes into maintaining the perception of law and bringing about convergence in this perception among many different persons. It requires enormous effort to keep this component of the instrument functioning and functioning effectively amidst changing conditions.

The third component of law we call lawmen, which includes lawgivers, sovereigns, lawyers, judges, legislators, and indeed any lawsayers, official or unofficial. People may believe such myths as law is a brooding omnipresence in the sky, but the fact is that as an instrument of conscious control law must be used by human beings. It makes little difference whether rules of law are thought of as being made or found, but they cannot be used effectively unless they are declared and brought to bear on situations. Any perception of law includes a notion of individuals who have a particular function or role and a particular status with reference to the law. Functional and status differentiation may be elaborate or simple but it is an integral component of the law. Lawmen may determine what shall be rules of law and rules of law may determine who shall be the lawmen, but this only suggests the organic or mechanical nature of the relation among the components of the law.

The role of lawmen in the law is well illustrated by two phenomena. First there is the notion of the lawgiver. In the Western world Solon of Athens is the prototype. Law was not then and is not now complete as an instrument of control unless there is someone to say what the law is, as a system, in the case of a lawgiver. Solon is thought of as giving to Athens not a particular collection of rules but rather a new legal system that was regarded as being especially useful for the culture of Athens. In addition to lawgivers there are those who perform various roles in the operation of the instrument. In modern times the idea of an individual lawgiver like Solon has given way to the notion of a sovereign as the lawgiver. Again this only indicates the necessity for the functional role of human beings in the law. The general structure of lawmen in modern times will be developed subsequently.

The fourth and final component of the law is jurisdiction. By definition rules of law must apply to limited situations; that is a perception must have form in order to be distinguishable and it therefore must have boundaries. Lawmen must operate within these boundaries or limits. In the broadest sense *de facto* jurisdiction is any set of limits within which law is an effective instrument. In a general sense, any instrument has a component similar to jurisdiction. A hammer is not useful for taking cinders out of a person's eye, and a ruler will not weigh wheat. To find what the jurisdiction of a legal system is, is to find the point beyond which it is not effective in controlling behavior. The hard and fast territorial boundaries most polities have nowadays are mainly boundaries between jurisdictions of law. Properly understood, law as an instrument would be as ineffective without jurisdiction, as without rules, perceptions, or lawmen.

Thus we see that in order to use law as an instrument to arm himself for greater effectiveness, any controller must know how to manipulate rules, perceptions, lawmen, and jurisdictions. He must get a lawman to declare a rule, get this rule perceived as a rule of law, and establish the limits within which he wants to and can use law to magnify his capacity for control.

In the final analysis, law as an instrument of control depends on the functions it performs with reference to the basic problems of control. Ultimately an individual using law as an instrument must move people. We turn now to an examination of how law facilitates the uses of coercion, persuasion, and proof in its operations.

The methods of control have been hypothesized as means for producing varying qualities of discomfort which can be deliberately created and varied for one person by another. The question then is how does law help man to utilize and give guidance to coercion, persuasion, and proof.

It has been argued that indiscriminate coercion produces, not control and achievement of purposes, but chaos and nihilism. Law serves to help man limit coercion and by limiting coercion to use it strategically and selectively. In order to avoid the indiscriminate production of intense discomforts by anybody and everybody against anybody and everybody, man uses the structure of rules, perception, lawmen, and jurisdiction in applying intense discomforts. Probably law is used universally to restrict those who use coercion to control others. As long as law commands respect or deference coercion is thereby limited, despite the fact that there are always many persons who would like to use coercion in order to achieve some goal. Coercion is probably universally permitted, but only in accordance with specific rules, made by specific persons and applied within determinate limits by specific persons. The hallmark of a rule of law is not that it has force or coercion behind it, but that because law is the most generally applicable control instrument it is customarily used to control the production of severe discomforts. When it is uncontrolled, coercion is the greatest disorganizer of human society. Since it apparently cannot be eliminated the problem is to control it, and nothing less than a legal system will enable man to do so.

Only man has intentions and purposes. The instrument of law aids him in achieving these intentions and purposes both by getting people to respond to law as law and then to the human purposes reflected in the law. Persuasion—the control method that produces less intense discomforts and secures less radical modifications in behavior—exploits an individual's orientation to beliefs, images, values, cognitions, and the like. In the broadest sense it involves the use of incentives and inducements that move people to appropriate action.

Despite much belief to the contrary, law is mainly an instrument for persuasion. As an individual matures he gradually forms a perception of law and thus acquires a feeling about its ethical and aesthetic components. If the perception-maintaining operations here have been effective in the polity, this feeling is one of respect, deference, and obligation. The individual is disposed to obey the law, which includes obeying those who speak in the name of the law—that is have their voice magnified, as it were, by the law. Because the individual respects the law, he tends to feel uncomfortable when he contemplates an act that is contrary to law. He is also uncomfortable when he observes other persons acting without respect for the law. Thus we say that he is effectively persuaded to conform to the rules of law, to maintain his perception of and respect for the law, to defer to lawmen, and to recognize the jurisdictions that are defined by lawmen using rules of law.

A controller uses law to persuade men to permit social security to be deducted from their pay checks. Fear of coercion may play a marginal role, but fear of lawlessness is probably more vital in the mind of the person who might be tempted not to yield to persuasion. Law is not effective when each person makes up his own mind; a polity cannot exist when each member makes up his own mind about everything in detail, for no purpose can be achieved in the absence of an overall pattern. Man without the instrument of law is helpless before the disorganizing forces of the universe. Having in mind purposes he wants to accomplish and states of being that he wants to maintain he is persuaded to support the law and thus use it for the accomplishments of his purposes.

Proof—the control method that produces the least discomfort and is capable of effecting the least radical behavior modification—is, in its pure form, a method in which the controlled comes to accept the controller's prescription as his own self-prescribed course of action. It is, we might say, persuasion with conviction instead of persuasion without conviction. In order to be moved to a course of action by proof, a person must be emotionally committed to the process of proof itself. If there is a firm commitment to the process, then the results are adopted and an act becomes in fact an act of one's own will.

Law converts proof into a useful means of control mainly by specifying and gaining acceptance of the particular process of proof. In other words, it establishes the conventions of proof, specifically, formally, and effectively. The clearest illustration of this is a criminal trial. Rules of law and lawmen are supported by appropriate perceptions and jurisdictional definitions in order to declare and guard the integrity of the process of proof applied to a question of whether a man has or has not violated a rule of law. Deference to the law secures deference to the process of proof prescribed in the law. The objective is simplified and made manageable, the variables are reduced and contained, and systematic steps are taken in order to depersonalize the process so that the same findings will emerge regardless of who uses the process.

In many of its uses, as has been indicated, the law does not apply proof in any great degree. This is a recognition that there is a limit to the usefulness of proof in securing control. The general consequences of a rule, for example, do not have to be proved before the rule is put into operation. Hence, although evidence may be introduced into a legislative hearing on proposed legislation, nothing like full proof is required. By definition, a rule has general applicability to a general range of situations, and the objective and the variables are too great and too complex to make a demand for complete proof before action. For a specific individual's alleged violation of rules, however, proof is useful, although many people feel it is a slow, laborious, and ineffective way to deal with violators of the law. The tendency to discard or set it aside as a means of control in times of crisis testifies to its frail nature in a turbulent state of affairs. Nevertheless commitment to a process which requires that those who decide important conflicts do so pursuant to proof is important and finds extensive use in the jury system.

Proof also performs another function in the operations of the law. As we have seen, the most powerful addition that law makes to an individual's control capacity depends upon the creation of respect for the law as such. One element in this creation is the perception of the law as an instrument of justice. No aspect of man's use of law for control purposes does more to give content to the image of law as justice than does the use of the specified process of proof for deciding individual disputes.

Law exists in all polities, but its effectiveness as a control instrument varies from polity to polity and even within one polity. We may say, however, that to the degree that law is effective in any place and at any time, it is because as an instrument it converts into operational practices the basic methods of control. When law is effective it represents a skillful blending of all methods, or of all degrees of discomfort, and in the hands of a masterful controller it does so in a selective and purposeful manner. With this in mind let us now turn back to the components of the law and examine some of the differentiations and refinements that are to be found within each component. This will give a better idea of the subtleties and general usefulness of law as an instrument of control.

Rules of law, as we have seen, are prescriptions of appropriate behavior in specified situations which are vested with the prestigeful designation of law. Rules may be differentiated in three ways: by sources, objects, and processes.

In practice, one way of specifying the rules of law and differentiating all other rules is by designating the source whose rules are to be considered as law. This has nothing to do logically with the content of the rule. Special deference-evoking qualities have been secured for rules by attributing their origin as rules to God, to nature, to kings, to sovereigns, to judges, to high priests, and to representative legislatures of one kind or another. In any polity where there is a well-developed system of law there is a whole gradation of laws (rules in terms of their source, and with the relation between the sources specified). For example, in the United States, there are laws by constituent assemblies or by popular referenda. These rules are generally called constitutional rules and are regarded as overriding any conflicting laws promulgated by other sources of the law. Then there are legislative or statutory rules, executive rules, administrative rules, and judicial rules. Thus the rules given legal quality emanate from different but always determinate, stable, and interrelated sources. This makes it possible to adjust them more precisely to the requirements of the particular control situation. At the same time it opens up all kinds of opportunities for conflicting rules and for blurring the image of the law. This is largely avoided, however, by the understandings of the lawmen and by the manipulation of the jurisdictional component.

The sources of law will vary among different cultures and subcultures but the very greatest importance will always be attached to the question of sources. The reason for this is not hard to find. As has been shown, for the quality of law to add anything to a rule it must be able to secure compliance in the face of opposition, dislike, and indifference. An individual rule must be obeyed not on its merit alone, but because it is law. In an effective system of law most people probably have to obey most rules on the basis of their merits, but legal quality adds a specific margin of control effectiveness by making acceptance more general and automatic. This being the case, one clear and simple way of vesting a rule with legal quality is to require that all rules emanating from a specified source be law, or rules of law. To make this effective a respect for the source of law must be developed and spread widely in the polity. One time it may be the gods speaking through medicine men or priests, next a king approved and even designated by God, and at still another time it may be the elected representatives of the people. To be effective law must come from a respected source. The basis of respect will vary with culture and situation. However, the source must also be specific and determinate. To the extent that law is effective there will arise no confusion as to what is and is not the rule that has legal quality.

Rules of law are also distinguished by the objects and behavior to which they apply. We do not have to list these, but we should note that in an effective system of law there is a structure to the grouping of rules, and that through these groupings consistency and precision are sought. To study any polity it is helpful to delve into the objects and behaviors that do not have any applicable rule of law. This is also a good perspective from which to study the limits of the effectiveness of imparting legal quality to a rule. Law as law is not effective where people follow particular legal prescriptions regardless of whether they are legal rules or not. It is also ineffective where a legal rule is properly promulgated as a prescription but where the people do not follow the prescription. In a dynamic society there are always arguments about which matters can be regulated by legal rules. Respect for the source of law may be diminished by rules that are widely resisted. Prohibition is one example, and the contemporary problem of civil-rights legislation is another.

There is another distinction about rules of law. This has to do with the process through which rules are given legal quality, and it is closely related to the matter of the source of law. Regardless of who the rulemaker is, he tries to avoid the impression that the rules are made up out of his own head on the basis of whim or caprice. Thus there is the tendency for rulemaking to be surrounded with a stable and determinate process. In primitive polities these processes may seem like magic, ritual, and ceremony, whereas in modern times the processes are defended as providing a guarantee of the rule's wisdom or its acceptance. Generally speaking, a rule is not regarded as a legal rule if the prescribed process for its adoption is not followed. Hence we do not expect the same rule to be as effective if it is adopted or promulgated without the process as it is if process requirements are met.

There is also a distinction between rules that apply directly to all persons in a situation and those rules which in effect apply to rules themselves. This merely calls attention to rules that specify the sources of law rules and the processes, and beyond this the whole field of public law, which primarily regulates lawmen themselves.

There is also a differentiation in the perception of the law. We have already spoken of the slightly different perception held by each individual who is conscious of and perceives the law. But beyond that there appear to be substantially different ways of perceiving the law, which vary among cultures, subcultures, groups, and classes in a polity. Some people perceive the law primarily in personal terms. That is to say that they personify the law by attributing human qualities to it, or they perceive it as a particular person, the sovereign or priest—"I am the law." Others may perceive it in inanimate terms such as documents, statutes, constitutions, decrees.

The phrase lawmen is used to single out those persons who use the law as an instrument of control and who are specialized in using law. In a given situation any person might be a lawman, as in the example of the man who used the law to stop someone from picking flowers. Where division of function is sharp, as in a highly developed system of law, distinctions are made between lawgivers, lawmakers, lawdeclarers or appliers, and advocates. The bench and the bar provide, of course, the clearest examples of professional lawmen. They may be said to specialize in the use of law as an instrument of control. A legislator, in so far as he is a lawmaker, also specializes as a lawman. Bureaucrats in general are regulated by law and use law in exercising control, but because they also use other instruments they are not so expert in the use of law as a specialized instrument of control. To the extent that they perceive the limits that the law helps impose upon their own control activities they are the objects of legal control, not the users of law on others.

The jurisdictional component of law may be further broken down into territorial, functional, and status jurisdiction. Where the effectiveness of law changes between persons living on one side of a line and those living on the other, we speak of the territorial basis of jurisdiction. Territorial jurisdiction has the instrumental virtues of clarity and simplicity. For example, a line marked on the surface of the earth can be specified accurately and can be found easily by standard methods. Not the least of the virtues of territorial jurisdiction is that it helps to minimize differences among the images held by the different people who respond to the law.

Jurisdiction based upon the particular character of interpersonal relationships is called functional jurisdiction. Within polities this is most clearly illustrated by specialized courts: admiralty, domestic relations, probate matters, small claims. This again only reflects the development of the law as a general instrument of control and the refinement of it for more precise control.

In some cultures there are jurisdictional distinctions based upon status, but in most polities it is hard to separate status and function. Children's courts and courts for different castes in a caste society are examples. Having different courts and rules for citizens and noncitizens is also an example of this jurisdictional distinction.

Generally, breaking down the components of the law reflects the refinement and specialization of the law as an instrument of control. This in turn suggests something of man's drive to clarify and shape his own more remote environment. The limits of law as an effective instrument for facilitating control and securing deliberately posited ends are determined primarily on an experimental or pragmatic basis. If the rules of law get so complicated that they cannot be followed, even by those disposed to follow them because they are law, if respect for the law lapses or declines for any reason whatsoever, if lawmen lose their skill, if jurisdictional boundaries become blurred and nonfunctional, then law loses its effectiveness.

When controllers press law into use to attain an end, and the end is not attained, there is a tendency to reduce generally, instead of selectively, the discomfort created by awareness of acting contrary to law. A vague awareness of this probably accounts for what many persons regard as the fundamental conservatism of lawmen in all polities. If their indoctrination and experience have created a perception of the law as something they feel an obligation to protect, then the law may be thought of as having a kind of built-in self-protection, reflecting the purposes of those who want to protect the instrument itself.

The law is generally the law of a polity, but law has its counterpart in all so-called private sectors of control; and as distance increases its special character more and more resembles *the* law. A so-called private controller operates by prescribing rules or norms of behavior which, if complied with, would help him achieve his control objective. If he can attribute such rules to an object that is appropriately oriented to by his potentially relevant respondents he can enhance their effectiveness. If he strives to attribute them to an association, these rules become the most general norms or prescriptions of behavior, limited of course to the jurisdiction of the association as it is perceived. As the size of associations increases, the visibility of the lawlike instrument increases, and there are constitutions, bylaws, officers, legitimating procedures, and the like.

Deliberate control of a more remote environment requires effective rules or prescriptions and the instrument we call law is designed to impart a special effectiveness to them. As distance increases, this special effectiveness becomes more and more necessary and the use of the instrument becomes more obvious.

Any conception of the law must be tested by its usefulness in explaining certain otherwise inexplicable observations. Something recognizable as law apparently exists in all interaction patterns in which the interactions embrace substantial spatial, temporal, or functional distances. The greater the remoteness, the greater the use of law and the more refined law becomes as an instrument. So the first great legal system was that of the Romans, who interacted amidst great diversity. Patterned interaction amidst such diversity does not come naturally. It is achieved by deliberate purpose in a polity in order to maintain a viable set of relations in the polity.

Law always seems to be surrounded with ceremony and ritual. This is so because these matters secure for the law that margin of additional control effectiveness and pervasiveness that distinguishes the law from moral philosophy and religious precepts. The law must be believed in even when people cannot see its good works, or when its works are not good or are regarded as not good. It must be capable of evoking feelings whenever it is introduced into the consciousness of man.

Indirectly the end of law may be justice, but because law is used for numerous ends that many persons do not regard as justice, this fact is not self-evident. Law is used to help regulate human action in accord with human will. If justice must be sought or made, rather than evolving naturally, then law can be used to secure justice. If justice is impossible where there is no deliberately imposed regulation, then too law may serve to facilitate the development and creation of justness in a polity. Otherwise we have to say that law is simply an instrument of control over a limited remoteness and that like all instruments it is limited as to the ends that it can help achieve. As it helps control human behavior it places limits upon those who use it as well as on those against whom it is used. By itself, however, this does not guarantee justice or the highest good, as the highest good is perceived by all persons.

Wherever law exists, where there is a consciousness of law as a distinctive phenomenon, it imparts a special effectiveness to human control of humans.

Law is always more pervasive in its accomplishments than would seem to be explainable by the presence of lawmen. It is an instrument that depends for much of its effectiveness upon the mere creation of awareness. One need not have a lawman standing at one's elbow in order to be aware of this. Law is universal because man by himself cannot create for himself a tolerable environment. He needs help—an extension of his personality. Thus through the ages he has invented and perfected law, for much the same reasons that he has invented and perfected the instruments by which he secures his food.

8

Agency

When a polity can be identified as a comprehensive bounded or limited "we" feeling, there can also be identified an object called law or legal system. Just as universally there can be identified such entities as ministries, departments, bureaus, commissions, parliaments, cabinets, congresses, parties, associations, groups, and the like. When any collectivity or interaction pattern is used as an object or entity by a controller to facilitate the achievement of a control end, it is called an agency. The word "agency" is used here to emphasize that the perspective in which we examine the lesser associations within the polity is that of a controller who uses these collectivities for purposes of that control we define as political. It is this instrumental perspective which has suggested borrowing the word agency from the law and appropriately modifying it. Its application as used here is by no means restricted to legal agencies or agency in law, but rather applies to any collectivity that is used or that can be used. Thus it is meant to bring under the term the politically relevant aspect of any collectivity, from an army to a family.

An agency comes into existence, or a collectivity becomes an agency, when in order to achieve a control purpose a controller requires help in making more detailed, accurate, and positive prescriptions of behavior and in securing acceptance of them. Thus, a congress by processing a proposed regulation refines, adjusts, and examines its contents and increases its control effectiveness by making the prescribed behavior more acceptable. A political party may facilitate the sorting out of officeholders and the articulation and aggregation of diverse interests. If the votes or support of a whole family can be obtained by persuading some member of it, then the family would be used as an instrument of political control and would be treated analytically as an agency.

We are here discussing agency from the perspective of the outside observer focusing on an interaction pattern that is a differentiated stage in a control continuum. The continuum runs something like this: from mover, controller, or initiator to a set of integrated actions which are distinguishable from the actions of the controller and from the end response which signifies the fulfillment of the control objective. Agency as an instrument of control is complemented by and complementary to law as an instrument, but it is distinguished from law by the relative narrowness of the control aspect it helps to achieve. Narrowness refers to number of acts, range of difference between acts, degrees of remoteness as heretofore defined, and positiveness of prescriptions. Agency enhances the effectiveness of a controller by increasing the probability of acceptance of more detailed prescriptions and by increasing the probability that such more detailed prescriptions are appropriate to the end sought.

There are three components of agency that require special

consideration. The first is its perception as an object by controller, contributor, and respondent; the second is its distinctive structure and process; and the third is its spokesmen or coordinators.

In order for an agency to enhance the effectiveness of a controller it must be perceived as an object, and the controller, contributors, and respondents must orient to the object in an appropriate manner. This orientation must be such as to predispose the controller to use the agency, the contributor to contribute appropriately, and the respondents to accept the guidance and cues promulgated in its name.

Upon perceiving or becoming conscious of a collectivity, an individual will orient to that object, and his orientation will have cognitive, affective, and evaluative aspects. He will have some understanding of the agency's operations, he will either be attracted to it or repelled by it, and he will tend to evaluate it in terms of other objects. To the degree that these aspects of his orientation are integrated, his behavior will be made more predictable.

The most tangible manifestation of the perception of an agency is its name. We might almost say that the name of an agency is one of its components, but the important thing is to understand why the name is so important in accounting for the agency's effectiveness as an instrument. Let us use two hypothetical examples. First, there is the employee who fits into the structure of the agency rather unconsciously and performs a task automatically. He receives his work from another person, makes his contribution, and then passes the work on to the next person, whose constant presence he never questions. This individual needs very little perception of the agency as a distinct entity. It is true that he must know the agency's name, its location, and the location of his own niche, and that he cannot know these things unless he knows one agency from another. The point is that there can be an employee who is barely moved by a consciousness, perception, or image of the agency as a discrete entity. We can say that this person's behavior is only minimally modified by his perception of the agency.

Essentially the same situation could exist among persons who did not work for the agency, but whose behavior modifications were the end objective of the controller for which the agency was used. A farmer, for example, may come to look upon a state employee as a personal friend and advisor and be quite unaware of, and hence have no perception of, the agency employing this man. Perhaps only when the particular agent is replaced by another does he become vaguely aware of the agency.

The foregoing suggests the other example. It is one in which either an employee or client clearly uses or responds to the perception of the agency. One employee might say to another that the prestige of the agency is low and the length of coffee breaks should be shortened. Or a farmer might say that the Department of Agriculture had reduced his acreage allotment. In these cases there is not only a difference in what is said, but also a difference in reason for the behavior. Any behavior that seems to indicate a concern for the agency as a whole can be explained by positing the presence of a perception of the agency as a whole entity. A farmer's awareness of Department of Agriculture policy might account for the modification of his planting plan, even though he had no reason to anticipate any adverse consequences if he did not comply with the Department policy. In this case, the perception of the agency would be an active component of the agency as instrument of control.

Earlier we noted that the practice of personifying agencies was about as universal as the existence of agencies. This attributing of personality and willed action to an interaction pattern is a shorthand way of expressing the perception of the agency. A remark is made that the Department of Agriculture wants a farmer to plant a certain crop. In reality, if course, the Department of Agriculture can want nothing of the kind: only human beings can "want" anything. Actually, the controller or some person in the Department wants something done; in order to increase the effectiveness of his request, he makes his request in the name of the Department. Of course, success depends on the respondent's perceiving the agency and being disposed to modify his behavior. Thus, what is spoken of as a willed actor is no actor at all, but rather the explanation of action. However, it is convenient and efficient to personify the agency, because then the request seems not the whim of an unknown and perhaps weak individual, but the desire of a wise and steady entity.

The nature of the perception of an agency is an important function of an agency and of agency users. If the perception of an agency is sufficiently sharp and is adequately affected, any individual speaking in the name of the agency can be highly effective. As we shall see, agencies primarily use persuasion as their basic means of control, and perception plays an important role in persuasion.

The controller also perceives and orients to the agency in a particular manner. His perception of the agency is manifested by such statements as, "I will turn this over to the Department," "We shall ask the Association to deal with this," "The party should adopt the following plank."

An agency has two distinctive but interrelated structures and a distinctive process that relates the two. One is a structure of discrete and limited action patterns, usually called roles, and the second is a structure of deference or authority, which has to do with making the various roles work together so that the agency will be a useful and precise instrument.

From the viewpoint of the controller, the attainment of any goal for which he undertakes to exercise control can be broken down into a series of intermediate control steps. This is always the case unless the goal is so limited and simple that the controller can accomplish it singlehandedly. When the intermediate steps are determined it becomes possible to divide up the work by assigning portions of it to the various persons who are cooperating with the controller. Therefore, one aspect of the structure of any agency is a system of roles, which, when performed, fulfill all the steps that are needed to accomplish the objective. A role may be defined as a task that can be performed by different persons according to a set prescription. Role structure can be observed in the operation of a factory. A worker who performs the same tasks day after day, without repeated instructions, can easily be replaced by another person, who will then assume his *role*. Thus, a structure of roles exists when the steps in an operation have been divided and the parts assigned with such definition that various persons can actually perform the task in accordance with the expectations of others. The first step for a controller who cannot alone exercise the control he aspires to is to create an agency; and the first step in the creation of an agency is the division and assignment of tasks or roles. These roles may be classified into those which help make the right prescription, those which help gain acceptance of the prescription, and those which primarily help to keep the agency functioning as an entity.

Role creation and assignment, however, is not enough to constitute an agency. Roles must be related to roles, or tasks to tasks; this does not come about by merely dividing and assigning the work. There must be developed what is known as a structure of deference. A situation must be created in which every role-player in the interaction pattern defers to the judgment of some other person or role-player; each one must set aside his own judgment and respond to the judgment of this other person in those situations where there is conflict or uncertainty. If there is no conflict, there is, of course, no need for deference: one does not need to defer to the judgment of his employer if he would do as the employer wanted him to do on the basis of his own judgment. Thus there must be a structure of authority so that in certain situations it is clear who makes the final decisions, who has the ultimate authority. Since an agency may involve many persons cooperating in the achievement of a goal, the various divisions must work together for the agency to serve its control function. Ideally, every agency must have a chain of command, so that the orders of the agency head can be transmitted through the various levels, eventually modifying the behavior of even the lowest employees.

Any agency has a special process through which it carries out its distinctive work, by relating tasks and deference in a functional manner. Agency process as a whole reflects the specific agency task of prescribing appropriate behavior and enhancing its effectiveness. This general process is made up of more specific but interrelated processes designed to collect relevant information, evaluate it, and to develop and choose between alternate prescriptions. There will also be processes designed to secure acceptance of the prescriptions, which will range from specific prestige-building processes to inspection, follow-up, instruction, negotiation. All of these subordinate processes tend to be specialized and to fit into what might be called the agency process, taken as a whole or a system.

What we have been characterizing as structure and process has largely to do with what is often called the internal affairs of the agency. In a sense the distinction between internal and external is only one of convenience. An agency actually comes to form an interaction pattern involving both the controller and the controlled. Nevertheless we do distinguish between the acts which are internally instrumental and those which are instrumental for the controller.

In addition to structure and process, an agency must also

have a component which serves primarily to relate the goal of the controller to the agency and in turn see to it that the agency is used for the accomplishment of the controller's final goal. The agency as instrument must as a whole be fitted to the task assigned to it. This function we are going to call co-ordination and it is one of the main components of an agency. It is variously called "leadership," "administration," in the broader sense of the term, and the "executive function." [1] We will call it coordination, not to be different, but because that word seems most aptly to describe the function that is performed.

The nature of the coordinator component is most clearly seen in a government department, where the constituents are often thought of as the controller. In this situation there is a rather inarticulate mass of persons in the position of controlling an agency which itself may be a fairly precise instrument. The coordinator must ascertain what is generally satisfactory to the controller and adapt the agency operation to it. He also must see that the final behavior modifications necessary for the achievement of the goal take place. This essential nexus between controller, instrument, and end objective does not come about naturally or accidentally; hence the necessity for the coordinator.

One of the more important aspects of coordination is to specify a spokesman for the agency. Since an agency cannot speak for itself, and since its processes are not carried out automatically, there must be someone who is recognized by controller, contributors, and respondents as the agency spokes-man.

The question may be raised as to why jurisdiction is not an agency component, as it is a component of the law. It is true that an agency is limited, but it is limited simply because it is a pattern. The conscious establishment and use of limits, implied in the notion of jurisdiction, is supplied by law for agencies and is the way agency is articulated with law. Thus one instrument is combined with another in the general process of control. But take the case of the so-called voluntary association, that is, one not given its jurisdiction from the outside. A voluntary association can be created and used for achieving purposes as long as those purposes and the interaction pattern are not unlawful. In this case the jurisdiction comes from the law. Short of such limits, the controller of the interaction pattern is in a position to use his instrument as he will and as he can. Jurisdiction of limits may be self-imposed for strategic purposes but it is scarcely realistic to consider jurisdiction as a component of an agency in the way jurisdiction is a component of law.

Thus we see that the agency's structure or process facilitates orderly preparation and dissemination of the contents of communications so that they contribute to the goal; the coordinator or spokesman keeps agency operations adjusted to the changing situation in which the goal is being achieved; and the perception of the agency helps predispose persons to follow the cues given by its spokesmen.

Having developed the components of an agency we are now in a position to explore further the process of creating agencies.

An agency, as we have seen, is a deliberately created interaction pattern which helps man establish control and thereby achieve goals. There are interaction patterns which appear not to be deliberately created. These are frequently referred to as natural associations or groups and are ones which do not arise primarily as instruments of control. It seems unlikely, as has been previously noted, that the universal existence of the family could be accounted for by hypothesizing its deliberate design for specific and limited purposes. It is equally hard to regard an army as a casual by-product of immediate and consciously perceived needs. It is true that any natural interaction pattern, so-called, may be used instrumentally for control purposes and to that extent it becomes an agency. The spokesmen for the Catholic Church, for example, rather explicitly use the family as an instrument of control. Political leaders use ethnic groups for the control of votes, or, more generally, to gain support for their actions. However, some interaction patterns are created primarily for instrumental purposes, and it is this phenomenon we are mainly concerned with when we consider agencies. Agency creation thus becomes relevant to the political theorist.

The creation of an agency requires first a notion of a particular control objective. For example, the objective of a police department is to control certain types of behavior. In addition, the controller or instrument-maker must be able to design a series of steps that will connect the controller with his desired end result. Generally speaking this requires two basic kinds of knowledge: knowledge of the culture within which the objective is to be pursued, and more general knowledge of some of the universal processes in human behavior. The latter knowledge is, of course, more basic: for example, a controller cannot create a step that would require people to work under conditions that are physically unendurable. The choice of incentives, however, must, for the most part, be worked out in terms of the culture: the controller must know what—a carrot, money, personal praise—will help elicit the behavior he wants.

The designer of an agency must also be able to prescribe role and authority structure suitable to the task at hand. And, finally, he must develop an appropriate perception of his agency and must specify the function of the coordinators with particular care for the entire control situation.

The following example should illustrate the process of agency creation: when the United States Congress decided to extend federal regulation over interstate railroads it also decided to create a new agency to make the regulation more effective. Thus, the controller and the creator—in this case,

Congress—combined the instruments of law and agency to create the Interstate Commerce Commission. Congress had passed a law prohibiting certain types of discrimination by carriers against shippers and declaring that rates charged had to be reasonable. Its purpose in creating the Commission was to make sure this law was systematically enforced. It prescribed an entity composed of roles and offices, provided a name for the entity, and established means for unifying and coordinating the operations of the entity in the field of transportation. It authorized the Commission to settle disputes and set new rates. Since this agency was created, certain individuals have exacted a special deference when speaking in the name of the Interstate Commerce Commission.

However, as it is used here, agency creation is not restricted to the creation of government agencies. The same kind of process is involved when a group of private persons create an interest group to facilitate control over a more remote environment.

A polity is, of course, always a going concern, and therefore what we have called agency *creation* is usually agency *modification*. But the principle is the same. A variation is deliberately introduced as a variation in an interaction pattern. To do this with confidence and certainty requires, as does agency creation, an understanding of the entire control process and continuum. The main point here is that intended behavior modifications for achievement of goals are possible, and the historical development of the agency phenomenon suggests infinite possibilities in this area. Therefore we should expect the same kind of inventiveness in this matter as we do in other areas of human activity and ingenuity.

A created agency is an instrument of control and we need now to consider how an agency is used for control purposes. An agency can be involved in two aspects of control, and these two will be treated separately. Because an agency is a pattern of interacting human behavior, the human behavior that constitutes the agency in action must first be controlled. This is one control problem. The second is the use of the agency to control behavior so as to accomplish the objective. In short, we must consider the control of the agency, and the control through the use of the agency.

In his study of the Communist party, *The Organizational Weapon,* the sociologist Philip Selznick has usefully developed the idea of an organizational weapon. Trying to explain its seemingly erratic behavior, he advanced the conception of the party as a kind of weapon that must be kept sharp so that it can perform any function that might be required of it in the future. This explains why its leaders always intervene in matters in a way that suggests that they do not really care about the outcome as long as they get experience and can weld the party faithful together into a cohesive and dynamic force. All agencies may be thought of as organizational weapons, although the sharpening of the instrument for future use may not be so distinct a preoccupation as in Selznick's conception of the Communist party.

No agency is so precisely defined and so rigid an instrument that it has one absolutely best way of doing everything. It operates within limits but with a certain tolerance between limits. Moreover, because it is composed of the discrete acts of whole persons it is subject to a certain lack of precision simply because of human differences. In fact, the more precise the work required of an agency, the more attention there must be paid to control *of* agency. The uses of a military force often require great precision, for example, in timing and in automatic response on a single cue. The control *of* an army, as distinguished from control *by* an army, is a matter of great concern and attention. Tradition, ceremony, practice, indoctrination, are exaggerated in an army, but it is important to bear in mind that they are only exaggerated and that their distinctiveness is only in the exaggeration.

In a very real sense an agency can be regarded as a set of predispositions or preparations. In the event that certain specified events take place, there are especially designated persons prepared in advance to intervene in a particular way. Thus the Interstate Commerce Commission is, in part, a set of preparations for responses to certain anticipated situations.

For obvious reasons, timing control, placement control, task-assignment control, authority-allocation control, competence control, are of fundamental importance to an agency's functioning as a control instrument. In short, there must be developed a sense of what the agency as an entity requires and this sense needs to be widely shared. To get a more concrete notion of what is involved in control of agency one can read the *Report of the President's Committee on Administrative Management* (1937) and the reports of the two Hoover Commissions, especially the first one. If, in reading the reports of these exhaustive studies of federal government operation, the President is thought of as the controller, the bulk of the reports may be viewed as dealing with the critical problems of agency control—that is, their control by the controller, not the control that is exercised through the use of them.

Because we have earlier distinguished between control of a near-at-hand environment and that of a more remote environment, we should note here that the problem of controlling an agency is essentially a problem of controlling a near-at-hand environment. This is to say that one is here dealing with greater functional, temporal, and spatial proximity. There is more stability and clarity in the structure; agency control is a daily not an occasional matter, and even if space intervenes in the pattern it is compensated for by greater functional definition and more limited time.

This lends some support to the often-made plea to keep politics out of the so-called internal affairs of an agency. The phrase "keeping politics out of an agency" usually means not using the agency for a control or instrumental purpose for which it was not intended. This may be illustrated by a few common occurrences. An agency is used for patronage appointments. To the extent that this modifies or affects the interaction pattern, the agency is being used to strengthen the effectiveness of another agency, usually the political party or the personal prestige of a man who has no direct functional relation to the agency. The agency is being used politically in this situation, for it is being used to secure an end not directly related to its explicit purpose. Although the phrase "used politically" is usually meant to be a criticism, this does not prevent it from being descriptive in the sense indicated. Another instance is the one in which a decision for promotion is made between two equally qualified people on the basis of a consideration outside the needs of the agency. The indirectness and lack of explicit structure in goal pursuit in these situations prompts the use of the term "politics." Of course, in the sense that an agency is used as an instrument to control a more remote environment, any agency is a political device. If we regard it strictly in its internal phase, however, typical political control methods need be used only to a limited degree.

In the final analysis an agency is used for, and has its existence justified by, helping to exercise control beyond its own component parts. A few words on this process are now in order.

In the United States a good example of agency's adding to law as an instrument of control are the so-called independent regulatory commissions. Before the passage of the National Labor Relations Act, for example, relations between employers and employees were regulated by law. The creation of the National Labor Relations Board provided another agency (in addition to the courts) to supplement the law. It helped provide standardized rules and regulations and to establish legal precedents.

Generally speaking, an agency is used to modify behavior either by operating directly on the minds of those whom the controller wants to control, or by helping to change a situation so that a certain change in behavior will follow. At the heart of the first method is communication. The agency may use rule prescription, orders, instructions, standards, education, propaganda—any of innumerable methods to introduce discomforts into the consciousness of the respondent. The Internal Revenue Service, for instance, exercises much of its function by direct communication with the individual taxpayer.

Other agencies, however, operate on behavior only indirectly, by changing the situation for the respondent. The most obvious examples here are those that involve construction of physical facilities. When there is a need for goods to be moved more rapidly and with greater safety, a highway department builds roads and installs safety features in the construction, rather than issuing directions for a speed-up of warnings about safety precautions. Similarly, changing the supply of money for circulation is a situation change which in turn leads to a change in behavior, usually of a predictable kind.

Actually, of course, most agencies act both on the respondents and on their situations, and it should be kept in mind that the distinction between the two is not a fundamental one. A communication may be thought of as changing the perceived situation for an individual, and when that individual's perception is changed, the situation is changed. Nevertheless there is a certain usefulness in the distinction we have drawn of the methods by which agencies serve to enhance the effectiveness of the controller. And the instrumental quality of an agency is made all the more clear by a realization that the agency methods are exactly the ones a controller could use were he powerful enough. An agency merely magnifies a controller.

It remains now to say a few words about the manner in which an agency uses and refines the basic control methods: coercion, persuasion, and proof.

In a well-developed polity, law is the instrument that guides most of the coercion for control purposes. There is, however, a tendency for law to run behind in its regulation of coercions, and thus controllers using agencies are often capable of performing coercive acts in pursuit of their goals. For example, many agencies that distribute benefits often find themselves inflicting discomfort as severe as that of well-regulated coercion when they withdraw these benefits for some reason. Police departments and military forces have an especially wide latitude in the use of coercion, and in these cases the agency design is such that the coercion is refined and specialized so as to achieve specific control objectives.

Persuasion, of course, is the primary means of control used. The most distinctive quality of agency persuasion is the new perception that is created when an agency is brought into existence. People are brought to a course of action in many cases because of the prestige of the agency in whose name the communication is issued or situational modification made. Thus the government-inspection stamp on a piece of meat often modifies behavior because of the confidence people have in the government or in the particular inspection agency. Obviously this kind of stamp is more influential than a manufacturer's stamp, assuming, of course, that respect for the government is greater.

One of the most important ways an agency uses persuasion is to develop a notion in the minds of the persons whose behavior it wishes to influence of what the agency spokesmen will do under certain conditions. This is to say that part of the perception that is developed includes a forecast of a certain type of action. In the light of this forecast behavior is often modified to conform to what is believed to be the agency's requirements. This is accomplished primarily through the agency's articulation of the policy of the controller.

Agencies also use various kinds of incentives in order to affect behavior. In addition to benefits, agencies may use awards, appeals to patriotism, citizenship, loyalty, conformity, authority, and similar attachments which, if considered simply by themselves, would scarcely be the grounds for the particular behavior modification.

Proof is also used by agencies. If the formula is clear, an agency can prove to a taxpayer how much he owes, and he can use proof to get one amount rather than another. Many of the inspections undertaken by agencies rely largely upon proof. Agencies often set standards of proof in various fields, but their acceptance depends upon the prestige of the agency as well as upon the practicality of the standards that are set.

A final word should be said about the use that has been made of the distinction between the controller, the agency, and the respondent. In a political system—the control system in a polity taken as a whole—all control tends to have a reciprocal character. A controller in one situation may be a respondent in another. And the reciprocity may make it difficult to distinguish between controller, agent, and respondent. In order to understand the control phenomenon, however, we must postulate the distinction. It hardly needs be said that in empirical investigations one should require evidence for the identification of the controller. It is no longer sufficient simply to locate the formal or prescribed controller. In distinguishing the controller from the agency it is probably a safe rule to characterize the controller as the person or group which has the last say, either negatively or positively. This kind of identification, of course, always involves a forecast based upon experience in similar situations. One could characterize the

President of the United States as the normative controller of the State Department, and one could probably establish the kinds of situations in which, both through anticipated reactions and actual presidential decisions, he is the controller. There is also a situation in which the President does not in fact have the last say, or at least does not use it. The person with the last say must be located within the agency, so to speak; he is then the controller, and the rest of the various components of the agency are the instruments he uses in order to exercise control.

It is obviously easier to characterize the President as a controller than it is Congress, for example: it is easier to think of one person rather than a group as a controller. But the distinction still stands. Initially, the majority that passed a bill is the controller, but once the law is passed it is appropriate to think of Congress as a whole as the controller. On questions of who shall sit in Congress, voters of the various constituencies have the final say, and in this area they are the controller, although the kind of control they can exercise is sharply limited by their indeterminate character. At the other end of the control continuum, the respondent is the person who must perform an act to complete the objective. The respondent is identified by the degree to which his behavior modification results in conformity with the action that the controller sought to secure. The intended respondent becomes the controller when he exacts conditions for his conformance either directly or by the controller anticipating the conditions for his response. Any formal or normative controller thus may also be a respondent in a reciprocal relation. Thus we talk meaningfully of control by and control of the government, or control by and of the President.

Agencies as they are treated here are not confined to political affairs. Because of the nature of politics, however, the agency instrument is exaggerated in politics, and thus we may say that there is a preoccupation with agencies in the study and practice of politics. One man is relatively helpless in the task of trying to impose control over his more remote environment, and so he must press other persons into the service of his cause. But they can be helpful in achieving common goals only if they are organized. This means that much of the control we call political involves agencies. Until the development of big business there was probably more concern with all aspects of agency creation and operation among politicians than among other persons. The models of agency creation have always been political agencies. The military has played an especially important role here because it has always created agencies that utilize many persons for a unified purpose and it has had to maintain a high degree of precision in its operations. The other great source of agency creation and use has been the churches, especially the Roman Catholic Church.

9

Agent

In the two previous chapters law and agency have been treated as instruments of control. In the present chapter we take up the third important instrument, which we call agent. Law as an instrument is distinctive by virtue of its generality and its impersonal nature. Agency finds its main use in control where the control or regulation requires more specificity and somewhat less impersonality than the law. An agent is any person whose behavior and status are used by a controller as a step in a process of imposing control over respondents. For example, it is customary for the President of the United States before personally offering an office to an individual to send an intermediary to sound out the prospective appointee and to persuade him to accept the appointment. For the most part nothing is prescribed in the law, nor is there any agency or office especially responsible for this kind of operation. The intermediary is an agent used for control purposes by the

President. This kind of extra-legal and extra-agency operation in a control system is widely used, especially where the element of remoteness is substantial. It is here regarded as the third main instrument of control.

Not all human control relations are legal or hierarchical, and some aspects of all control relations are nonlegal and non-hierarchical. The key to a control problem in many cases will be in an area where general relations have no preexisting and stable structure. These are the areas where personalities, rapid situational change, and the need for highly specialized competence enter into the control picture. Here negotiation, bargaining, give and take, balance, adjustment, and compromise play a large part in the control process. Just as a military service is a model of all agencies, so the field of diplomacy—relations between polities—finds the clearest use of the agent, although the agent is a complementing instrument in all control undertakings.

As an instrument of control an agent may be thought of as the combination of three components: personality, assignment, and perception.

Personality is that relatively stable blend of all characteristics and qualities which distinguishes one person from another. Within an agency, roles are assigned ordinarily with personality factors in mind, but roles and role-occupants are interchangeable in an agency. A substantial tolerance of personality differences within the same role is necessary. This tends to reduce the possible exploitation for control purposes of the personality or total person. One of the main steps in the use of an agent as a control instrument is to select the personality to fit the specific control problem faced, without special regard for the appropriateness of that personality in other control situations. The personality component of control instruments increases in importance as one moves from law through agency to agent. Law depersonalizes control; agent personalizes it.

The second component of agent we shall call assignment. Because an agent is always the agent of some controller or some principal, there can be no agent without an assignment. The assignment helps the agent increase his effectiveness, for it gives him a sense of legitimacy and confidence about his mission. Assignment is also important because of the effect it has on the immediate person or collectivity whose behavior is to be modified as a step in the control process. Appropriateness of assignment is a part of an agent's effectiveness that does not depend upon his personality or his behavior. Rather it establishes his status.

The third component of agent as instrument of control is perception—that is, perception of him as an agent. The perception of an agent must be such as to maximize his effectiveness with two perceivers—the controller and the respondent—and it is in satisfying the two perceivers that the importance of perception is brought out. The controller must perceive his agent as one he can trust. The agent must be able to use his own judgment in full confidence that the controller will approve and support his decisions. To be effective as an instrument, the agent must be able to speak for the controller or principal in unanticipated situations.

In addition, the agent must be perceived by the respondent in such a way that the effectiveness of control is increased. The qualities that make an agent suitable for the controller may make him ineffective against the person to whom he is sent. There is a rather formal acknowledgment of this in diplomatic relations: for example, a prospective ambassador must be cleared by the country to which he is appointed. The formality of this example, however, should not obscure its common use in control systems. The function of an agent, it should be emphasized, is different from that of a courier or messenger. The agent must evoke deference from the respondent beyond that evoked by the controller. Where agents are necessary, margins are highly important. The agent must be a person who is positively perceived by both ends of the control relation. Thus the instrument we call agent requires the most precise and delicate use of the arts of politics.

Now that we have developed the idea of the components of agent as an instrument of control we can turn to a consideration of how agents are controlled and how they are used to control.

A controller must control his agent before he can control through his agent. The difficulty of this stems from the very qualities that make an agent effective. He must be regarded as speaking for his controller or principal. In order to be effective with the respondent he is always tempted to overcommit his controller. Much of the control of agents is exercised in selecting them. In an agency, training ranks with selection as a method of control, but for an agent training is of less importance.

The assignment process—one of the essential components of the instrument we call agent—may also be used to maintain control over the agent. In considering the use of assignment for control purposes it is important to bear in mind the control need that requires the use of agent. The immediate control target is a person or small collectivity, but the end objective is a more remote environment. The purpose is to modify the behavior of the immediate control target as a step in securing a modification of more remote behavior. The agent needs to understand not only the policy and general objective of his principal but also how the immediate control target relates to the ultimate required behavior. If the assignment step is used to clarify and make explicit the end result sought, it will tend to effect a control over the agent finely adjusted for the task at hand. Since the problems requiring the use of agents often involve compromise and bargaining, it is also important that the agent understand what cannot be given up in the process.

In a polity that is stable and systematic in exercising control, law is used to regulate and apply coercion. Thus we would not expect a controller to make much use of the other instruments by themselves, especially when control requirements seem to suggest the application of coercion. But not all polities are stable and systematic, and, depending on the particular culture and situation, control requires many intricately related acts. An instrument such as the law, for example, imposes certain limitations upon the controller who uses it. What is a controller to do when he feels, justifiably or not, that he must use coercion to accomplish an end but finds that the law does not permit coercion in the situation or that it would be too slow and ponderous for him to follow legal prescriptions? Generally speaking, he will try to give an aura of legality to his act. It is here that he is likely to press an agent into service. The use of blackmail or threat by a controller—coercions that most law systems are incapable of applying—is usually handled through an agent. Obviously such uses of coercion without legal prescription are usually found in an unstable or revolutionary situation.

Nevertheless, there is always some tendency for controllers who become intent upon the achievement of their goals to use coercion, and the borderline between coercion and noncoercion, as we have seen, is a thin one. There are many instances in the United States in which local bosses and political machines use agents to apply coercion. When the controller uses an agent to apply coercion he usually tries to avoid involving the law in the control effort. This is because the law more or less automatically controls many types of behavior that any controller wants controlled. But this kind of control is dependent upon a widespread feeling that law is used for limited purposes and operates by known means. Acts that destroy confidence in the law render it ineffective as a control instrument. If the bond of law snaps, even the most ardent revolutionist would not want to contemplate the consequences. This accounts for the tendency in certain situations to use agents as the sole instrument in the application of coercion.

All control of a more remote environment, as we have seen, depends largely upon some form of persuasion. The persuasion of the law is based largely upon the perception of the law, and respect for the perception as a source of high priority prescriptions. Thus a rule of law secures compliance just because it is the law. The distinctive persuasional base of an agency is the perception of the agency, but it is more selective and depends upon a more or less separate perception of each agency. Thus agency does not have the generalized persuasive capacity that the law has. The capacity of an agency to modify behavior is more dependent upon its function and the services it renders. In both law and agency an impersonal object stirs the feelings. This explains why law and agency are so indispensable in extending uniform behavior over a more remote environment.

The persuasional basis of the agent is distinctive because it is more personal than that of either agency or law. Compliance is secured more on the basis of the agent's personal qualifications. An agent's use of persuasion is, of course, dependent upon the personal likes and dislikes of the respondent, his perception and understanding of the relation of the agent to the controller, his readiness to respond to expertness: it is dependent upon the respondent's perception of the specific situation.

The agent is able to modify behavior by the use of persuasion in ways that depend less upon the perception of him and the feelings aroused by the perception. This is true because he operates on a more personal level, and he can tailor his appeal to the particular person or group he is dealing with. Prejudices, predilections, and predispositions that might first

appear completely irrelevant can often be pressed into persuasional service by the agent. Thus, as a control scheme is
spread over an environment that extends from the proximate
to the remote, the agent, by his use of persuasion, is important
in establishing a link between the near and the remote. He
thus tends to round out any control scheme by serving as a
complementing instrument.

There is frequently a feeling in politics that the establishment of a personal connection can win a control objective that
could not otherwise be achieved. This reflects the conviction
that personal attractiveness, prejudices, predilections, and
predispositions can be effective. But it also sometimes reflects
the belief that in such a setting it may be possible to press
proof into service more effectively. Whenever international
tensions develop there is usually a call for top-level talks,
prompted by a belief that the principals or their immediate
agents can ease tensions by talking things over. In personal
conversation it is possible to bring out the points of resistance
and to subject them to standards of proof.

Summit meetings often reflect a naïveté about the limits of
proof in the face of strong resistances to modification. But
they also reflect a truth about the conditions under which proof
is likely to be effective in modifying behavior. Proof must be
capable of using evidence to sweep away all objections. Proof
in practice is a chain or sequence of proofs. Unless one knows
the objections and resistances of the respondent it is never
certain that all objections have been swept away, even where
it may be possible to prevail if the objections or prejudices are
known and subjected to the proof process. Thus, as we have
already noted, proof as a means of control is most effective
in clearly delineated situations, and in a setting where the unanticipated objections may be brought out and answered.
From this we might expect that proof as a control method
would lend itself well to an agent. This may help to account

for the extensive use of agents in international dealings. The ordinary bases of persuasion do not exist in the sense of being shared among nations. And in international affairs, the use of coercion tends to mean the chaos of war. Thus, despite its frailty, it is essential to use proof as much as possible and in the most effective manner. Because objects of strong and common loyalty between polities are weak, they do not provide a basis for the use of persuasion. The United Nations evokes some loyalty but it is relatively weak in this respect.

Law, agency, and agent are thus the three primary instruments used to control and regulate a more general and remote environment. One would expect to find them being used in any polity with a viable and flexible control system.

The effectiveness of control means and instruments, however, does not depend only upon the methods and instruments. Their effectiveness is also shaped by the character of the control problem upon which they are used, and this is determined by the nature of certain fundamental relations among people. We next turn to a consideration of these fundamental relations as they affect and are affected by the control system.

FOUR

Response and Resistance to Control

The foregoing discussion has concerned itself mainly with control and controllers. The character of response has been dealt with only as it was incidental to making clear the pattern of control behavior. However, acts do not have control consequences without responses; empirically the character of response feeds back to the controller and modifies the control acts. Hence control systems are shaped as much by response patterns as they are by the intended patterns of control acts. To complete a discussion of the control system we call political we must now turn our attention to the response side.

Response to control acts is always a response by an individual, and there may be as many different responses as there are individuals. The character of the actual responses can only be known empirically but it is the task of theory to suggest the probability of general response patterns.

A response to a control act is made up of several components. First there is the individual per se, or what might be called the individualistic element, which accounts for the similarities as well as the differences in all individuals. Similarities shared by the species limit and facilitate responses. On the other hand, we may say that each response to a control act will be in some respect different from all others. Responses and response patterns will be shaped in part simply by the essential nature of what is responding, regardless of grouped differences. Thus, we take up first the question of the significance for response of the fact that a respondent is an individual human being. The sample of the human species differentially affected by any polity or political control system is sufficiently large to represent both universal differences and similarities. For this reason we should expect that responses would be similar and similarly varied between political control systems and all other control systems. We should also expect that political writings and practice would manifest an enduring concern with the place of the individual per se in the system.

Only individuals respond to control acts, but the individual's response is in part shaped by his orientation to other relevant objects in his environment. These objects may be inanimate objects, animate objects (including other individuals), or interaction patterns which are perceived as objects and are oriented to. They may also be ideologies, myths, cognitive systems perceived as objects. When these objects are perceived as relevant—that is, affected by or affecting the response to a control act—they may be said to act as an intervening and shaping force in the response and response pattern.

A definitive theory of politics would have to explore each of these separately in order to conjecture about the special character of each as it mediates and intervenes. For present purposes, however, we shall deal with these in more general terms.

Just as respondents, being human, impart some of the shape and substance to a control system, so perceiving and orienting in various ways to groupings of individuals imparts a special shape to responses. In short, there is something universally characteristic in the act of orienting to a group, or social formation, as we prefer to call it. Hence we shall explore the effects of groups or social formations per se in shaping responses to control.

Experience shows that politics is enduringly and universally concerned with individuals and with groups. But it also reveals that persons both as individuals per se and as individuals shaped by objects in the environment reflect certain enduring concerns highly relevant to politics. We cannot assume that these enduring concerns are a mere coincidence, and therefore we must explore the nature of this persistence. These concerns are other polities, religion, and economics. Each is at once a factor in the individual psyche and the basis of distinctive groupings. Hence when we discuss religion we shall deal with the individual's concerns which gives rise both to religious doctrines and to religious groups. The same is true of the world of the economy and the world of polities. We shall now turn to a consideration of how individual concerns respond to and shape control action.

10

The Individual and Polity

"The most persistent of all political questions is this: To what extent or in what spheres may government properly control individual conduct?" [1] This statement is readily accepted by most students of politics, but a most searching examination must be made to find out why this persistent question has not been answered successfully.

Because we are now discussing control from the respondent's viewpoint, our attention is focused upon a single act of a single person. We may assume without proof that not all of any person's acts are wholly controlled, deliberately or otherwise, by other persons or forces. This is merely an application of the basic assumption that all men to some degree determine their own acts. Thus it is useful to think initially in terms of *controlled acts* rather than in terms of controlled persons or actors.

We shall refer frequently to individuals acting but it should be borne in mind that this refers to specific acts, sets of acts or patterns of acts that are fairly limited and simple. In this sense the act is the unit.

From the general perspective of control, the most appropriate focus of attention is the act that an individual performs pursuant to a cue from an external controller—an act the individual does not want to perform, or never thought of performing. It is in this type of situation that the control act can be more clearly separated from the response act. In general terms then, in order to separate control acts from response acts we must find a situation in which the probabilities are high that an individual will act in a specific way, or will not act at all. We can then try to account for a particular modification. We are particularly interested in those control acts that are an outgrowth of a deliberateness, conscious purpose or calculation on the part of some person whom we hypothesize as the controller. There are many acts of one person that produce an observable consequence that is often called control, but the ones we are interested in here are those which are deliberately undertaken and which effect a control of a more remote environment.

What is the range and nature of responses that an individual can make to a control act designed to modify his intended behavior? In the first place he may automatically comply and modify his act in the manner intended by the controller in using the control act. He may do this because he has developed a reflexive habit of following the cues automatically if they emanate from certain persons or sources. In this case we may say that the controlled finds less discomfort in following the cue of certain persons than in performing his original act. The extent to which there will be this kind of automatic compliance depends upon the relative strengths of the habit of deferring and the demand to persist in the original act.

At the other end of the scale, an individual may completely

refuse to modify his own acts. In this situation, no amount of discomfort could be worse than that involved in modifying his behavior.

On a scale between absolute, automatic compliance at one end and absolute intransigence at the other, a whole series of intermediate responses is possible. For example, there is the delayed response, in which the controlled person reorients his personality system to fit the modification into his ongoing overall pattern of action. There is also the adaptation to the control act and the stamping of the response with the respondent's own personality system. Further along the scale there are various degrees of deliberation which introduce an element of delay and lead to a modification of what the controller is able to impose. Still beyond this, there are evasion and protracted delay.

One constant in all of this is, of course, a system of communication between the controller and the controlled. The main symbol system is language, but the importance of non-language symbolism in communication should not be overlooked. Demeanor, gestures, signs made with the face and hands, as well as such symbols as uniforms, insignia, and knowledge of status role, are involved. A control act is dependent upon the existence of such a system at the time the control act is performed. To be effective control must take place in a situation where both the controller and the controlled share an understanding of communication symbols and of the situation. Generally speaking, the more remoteness there is between the controller and controlled the more they will depend upon the formal and explicit characteristics of the communication system. The remoteness factor in politics thus suggests why there is so much preoccupation with language and formal symbols, such as flags, insignia, and offices.

In addition to a scale of resistance on the part of the controlled, there are essentially two kinds of response, or two elements in any response that the controlled makes. One is adaptive or adjustive in nature. Here the controlled simply tries to escape the deprivations or discomforts by rearranging his own personality system. In the other type of response he may take measures of counter control. In the latter case he may try to make the controller modify the control act so that it is more in keeping with the preferences of his personality system. In this case the controlled becomes a controller. The control relation is thus reversed and control tends to become a matter of reciprocation. Patterns of control emerge over time and with experience and they become an integral part of the equipment with which any individual deals with his environment.

Countercontrol, like control, may take specific and general form. There may be efforts to reduce the *general* effectiveness of the controller by, for example, removing him from office. At the political level, elections are practices whereby specific controllers, rather than their acts, can be changed. Lobbying is an example of an accepted direct means of trying to change control acts or a control system. In all cases some combination of coercion, persuasion, and proof are used in countercontrol, just as they are used in control. Basically, the only difference between control and countercontrol is in the perspective of the controller. If he acts to control in response to previous or anticipated control gestures, it is countercontrol; if he initiates, it is control. For practical purposes the difference between an initiated control act and a responsive control act is highly important.

Any discussion of the relation between the control act and the response act leads into a concern with freedom and equality. This is especially true of the political component of general control.

First let us examine the nature of freedom from the perspective of the controlled individual and then look at the unique aspects of freedom in the political realm.

It is hard to see how freedom can be anything other than a subjective feeling. A man is free if he feels free. To experience a sense of comfort, well-being, and autonomy that one cannot imagine being improved upon is to feel absolutely free. But no man can be absolutely free in this sense because, if for no other reason, change is wrought by time whether man wills it or not. The very act of interacting with other persons produces changes to which an individual *must* respond. This alone deprives him of some measure of freedom. In short, one expends psychic energy in unintended ways in interacting with other persons.

In the perspective suggested here, control is related to freedom by virtue of the fact that a response to any control act must make some reorientation of a personality system. The least free person is one who is being bombarded with so many environmental changes, or with such drastic changes, that in responding he cannot maintain the integrity of his personality system. Inability to respond to control acts either through adjustment or countercontrol, and in a way that maintains the integrity of one's personality system produces terror. This is what is meant by a complete or nearly complete loss of freedom. Erich Fromm defines freedom as the ability of a person to preserve his integrity in the face of power.[2] More important for the individual, however, is his perception of his ability to preserve integrity in the face of power.

Complete control is as impossible as complete freedom. There is some tendency in discussing freedom to assume the existence of a fixed quantity of freedom that is depleted with each control act imposed. In this way freedom is regarded as a fixed and static thing, a substance that may be hoarded, added up, and subtracted.

Despite Fromm's very important insight expressed in the

title of his *Escape from Freedom* there is a sense in which he misconceives the nature of freedom. All of us in some phase of our lives get a real sense of freedom and well-being by following the control cues of other persons. Moreover, it is not *what* threatens the integrity of our personality system, but *anything that threatens it*, that deprives us of freedom. The masochistic tendencies that account for some persons wanting to escape what most other persons would regard as a sense of well-being and comfort are properly regarded as abnormal. One can find out if there is widespread freedom among a people by conceptualizing a model of a healthy, confident, vital personality system. Freedom is found where such personality systems are predominant in various levels of a society.

Freedom is not a fixed and possessed thing. It is a quality of life. And like action itself, it is something experienced only by individuals. If, in a given situation, it is invigorating and comfortable for an individual to initiate his own acts autonomously, the act resulting is a free act. It frees the individual. If, however, action or the prospects of choice result in a feeling of oppression and enslavement, then the act or choice taken is not free and has no freeing consequences. Effective control acts always create a discomfort, but the response to the discomfort may be creative and exhilarating and may produce a real sense of freedom and well-being. We know through research that some methods of control tend usually to be more unsettling and disturbing than others. Perceiving the dissolution or disintegration of one's personality or identity is generally more unsettling than being placed in a logically untenable position or in seeing possible harm to a loved object, person, image, symbol, or myth. Any control sanction, however, can be imposed so as to provide a greater or lesser threat to the integrity of one's own personality system. Threats to freedom, moreover, lie more in *how* control discomforts are imposed than in *what* act is controlled.

The widespread belief that arbitrary and terroristic acts are the greater threat to freedom is soundly based. Such acts assault the integrity of the whole personality system, and brainwashing may disorganize a personality system completely. We call fear the feeling generally aroused by a perceived direct threat to the integrity of a personality system. Coercion is any control act that is perceived as a direct threat and thus relies upon producing fear. Persuasion results in a more indirect and peripheral type of threat as perceived by the individual. Proof is a still lesser threat. But the most unsettling thing for the personality system is to be called upon to respond to control acts which do not "make sense." Any act that threatens a personality by producing discomfort is greatly intensified if the purpose of the threat makes no sense to the threatened person. This is true regardless of the means of control used. However, the process of proof is properly regarded as most solicitous of the personality system of the controlled, primarily because it assumes the *form* of making sense. Persuasion may be thought of as an indirect pressure, or as what Rousseau had in mind when he referred to persuasion without conviction. This is why it is often said that a custom-dominated society is basically a free society, or at least that in a governmental system that does not base control on the customs of the people, there is relatively less freedom.

Up to this point we have been discussing freedom in general. This has the double advantage of making the nature of freedom clear and calling attention to the fact that *threats* to freedom come from all control, deliberate and nondeliberate, political and nonpolitical. Before turning to the special case of the relation between freedom and control of the more remote environment, we must say a few words of explanation about the general demand for equality.

The claim to equality is often taken to negate the claim to freedom. A realistic understanding of the nature of freedom, however, shows that this is not the case. Rather it shows a close and intimate relation between the two. Take the individual whose personality system is being threatened or unsettled by the intervention of a control act. We have advanced the hypothesis that if the deprivation accompanying a control act "makes sense" to the controlled, it reduces the degree to which he views the deprivation as a threat to the integrity of his personality system and his freedom. Thus anything that tends to make more sense out of a control act will moderate any perception the controlled has of a threat to the integrity of his personality system. To see other persons similarly treated provides some assurance that there is sense in the deprivation. Observing how other persons similarly situated are treated provides a person with a check upon his appraisal of his own treatment.

Thus, the demand for equal treatment is an outgrowth of the demand for freedom. This is why different treatment for different persons based upon differences that a person does not perceive or regards as irrelevant is so disconcerting. The importance of how things are seen cannot be overemphasized. For example, the Negro sees himself being treated differently for reasons that make no sense to him. That is to say, once he rejects as irrelevant any basis for different treatment he feels enslaved. The white man in the South treats the Negro differently because he feels he is significantly different from him. But the Negro is beginning to reject the significance of the difference. A general claim to equality is a general claim for limiting the bases for different treatment. It is a claim that all controllers should accord different treatment only in cases where the differences are clear and significant. They should also try to leave a person's existing behavior patterns undisturbed by deliberate control acts unless the respondent can make sense out of the control act.

Why is freedom of the individual so often discussed with reference to politics? Is the kind of control we call politics a special threat to an individual's freedom and sense of well-being? Three aspects of politics are relevant here: deliberateness, the more remote environment, and the perceived unit.

First let us ask if a control act is likely to be more upsetting and disturbing to a personality system because it is deliberately undertaken by another person. Much nondeliberate control imposed on an individual is imposed by his physical environment. This tends to be relatively less upsetting because an individual gets used to the pattern and so is able to adjust to the changes that can be expected. A violent storm, of course, may terrify him, but in most of his day-to-day life he knows how to cope with the changes with no fundamental derangement of his personality system. In a sense this is also true of the undeliberate acts of his fellow men. Their patterns of behavior become familiar and he gradually gains experience to help him get along. When, however, he is subjected to the calculated control acts of other persons he is apt to be less prepared by experience and thus ask whether the control act is really necessary. He perceives the similarity between himself and the controller and attributes to the controller the same measure of free choice that he himself has.

Thus, we see that when a person perceives a control act as not being inevitable or unavoidable he is prompted to question compliance with it. The possibility of deliberate avoidance or of countercontrol explains why so many deliberate control acts are erroneously labeled as necessary, or as being the natural working of the universe. This is why effective controllers tend to claim that they speak in the name of the law or in the name of an office. Thus we must conclude that there is a difference in the capacities of deliberate control acts and nondeliberate ones to cause discomfort and anxiety about preserving the integrity of the personality system. The scapegoat phenomenon is a perverted form of the search to impose meaning on deprivations that do not actually make sense. If we perceive a control act as being deliberately imposed upon us it tends to be perceived as a threat and thereby reduces our sense of well-being.

A control act that reflects a deliberate controller's concern with his more remote environment has an even greater effect upon freedom. An act that produces politics is undertaken to produce consequences in persons who are remote and for ends that are remote. The politician may want to control the acts of more remote persons as a means of controlling his own immediate environment, but the resisting tendencies of the more remote environment make this difficult. It is true that the kind of act that results from a deliberate effort to control the more remote environment requires a certain discomfort and disarrangement in the form of releasing physical and psychic energy. But the very deliberateness and remoteness of the control permits the controller to regulate his behavior more deliberately in terms of his own deprivations.

All of this is to say that in acts designed to control the more remote environment there is a certain tendency to irresponsibility, a lessened concern about the adverse and inevitable consequences of acts. In acts by which an individual controls his more immediate environment, the controller is more readily and directly subject to countercontrol, even in the form of retaliation. "Knowing" a person makes it much easier to seek out the weak spots in his psychic armor and to take advantage of him. Thus, even from the perspective of the controller there is a difference between control acts in the remote environment and in the immediate environment.

When, however, one views matters from the perspective of the controlled person he finds that the control act is personal and immediate. Because the control act is intended to control a more remote environment of another person, it may be more difficult for the respondent to make sense out of the discomfort inflicted. The more remote the purpose and consequences of an act of compliance, the more difficult it is for the person who performs the complying act to make sense out of it. To a man who pays taxes, the deprivation is direct and immediate to his personality system, whereas the purposes for which the tax money is used is apt to be vague and remote. Thus it is that the deliberate acts to control the more remote environment are potentially capable of adversely affecting freedom in a high degree, and this is why in controlling the more remote environment there is so much use of justification and simplifying devices like myths and metaphors. If taxes can be satisfactorily justified as necessary to keep "Old Glory" flying high and if the taxpayer has developed a love for "Old Glory," the loss of freedom is discounted in large part.

The remote component of politics does indeed bear a special relation to the question of freedom, and the resistance to taxpaying is natural, explainable, and seemingly universal. People revolt against taxes when they believe the taxes are unfair in amount, purpose, or distribution. Inducing people to believe that they have consented, through their representatives, to pay taxes must be counted as one of the great myth-type inventions. It helps make possible and tolerable the human control of a more remote environment.

The perceived-unit component serves as a simplifying device and hence makes it easier to understand the reasons for what would otherwise be considered unreasonable demands. This perceiving of a unit, of course, operates in controlling all environments but, as we have previously indicated, it has a special importance in controlling the more remote environment. This is because some kind of a simplification of the more remote environment is especially necessary because of its comprehensive and complex nature.

Thus we must conclude that the age-old suspicion that politics has a special involvement with freedom is substantially correct. This is not, however, because politics is control, but rather because it is deliberate control of a more remote environment. This should serve to focus discussions of politics and freedom upon the nature of deliberateness and the special problems of controlling the more remote environment.

Before leaving the subject of control and the individual a few further observations are in order. From the perspective of the controller, every successful control act has two consequences. One is securing the intended behavior modification as a step toward achieving the end in view. The other consequence is helping to maintain the control system per se. The quality of a control act is always determined in part by the requirement that it contribute to the maintenance of the system. Form is an important outgrowth of this requirement. We see it most clearly in international dealings where protocol is of special importance. The controller must bear in mind how unintended by-products of one effective control act may influence the effectiveness of the next control act. Will one control act be executed in such a manner that the controlled will be disposed to comply with other control acts yet to come, the nature of which is undetermined? Another side of the same phenomenon may be observed where there is a great emphasis upon discipline, as in an army. Here a control act must be made to elicit a response, not merely to serve the immediate control purpose, but also to condition the controlled to follow orders. The habit of obeying must be instilled and constantly renewed, and any control act must be such that it contributes to the renewing and strengthening of this habit.

This phenomenon is similar to the system by which some of the earnings of business must be plowed back into the enterprise in order to keep it going. This is known as capital accumulation and has its counterpart in all control, since all control takes place in the framework of a control system. But just as it is not always easy to get people to save in order to accumulate capital, so it is not always easy to explain to the controlled why they must do something in order to maintain the control system. And if this is not clear to them, the act they are required to do may make correspondingly less sense and thus be more unsettling to their personality systems. Indeed so little is known about the essential nature of maintaining the control systems that it is difficult to gauge whether an act improves or weakens the system. Moreover, the lack of understanding about how to maintain the control system accounts for a large part of the conservatism in control acts and responses. It also accounts for the rather hysterical fears that are engendered by acts that are believed to be destructive of the system. People tend to be unwilling to take calculated risks where they feel wholly incapable of calculating.

Another observation is that theories of individual punishment change the nature of the control process. For example, a punishment based upon a theory of retribution and seeming to flow naturally from the notion of retribution will make sense as long as the theory is maintained and widely accepted as valid. But if the punished person and the rest of society come to accept a different notion of punishment, one therapeutic in nature, then acts of retribution are viewed as especially harsh and lacking in sense. The threat to freedom in this case is increased, not by any change in the act of punishment, but by a modified perspective. This is but another way of saying that the expansion and contraction of individual freedom is as much a matter of changes in the perspectives as it is of changes in the nature of the control acts or sanctions themselves.

Earlier we discussed agents and agencies of control. In most discussions of control there is a tendency to think of groups, associations, social formations, and the like as being subject to control in much the same way as individuals are. This usage, which has corporations and families claiming freedom, needs to be examined in order to ascertain in what sense it is possible to think of a group or a collectivity responding to control by a controller. This is the subject matter of the next chapter.

11

Group and Polity

There is widespread belief that groups of people, as opposed to separate individuals, are especially important in the field of politics. This is expressed in much of the literature of politics and in the writing and speaking of political leaders. We must examine this belief and try to determine the nature of group effect on response. In our discussion here we shall take "group" to mean any kind of aggregate, unless appropriately qualified.

Not only is there a widespread belief that groups are important, but there is also a tendency to attribute to groups the characteristics of an actor. Groups are said to do this or that, to act in various ways. Individuals and groups are often treated as if they were quite interchangeable. This tendency must also be examined and explained.

There is a basic distinction between two phenomena each of which is generally called a group. Both are relevant to politics but one is of special importance from the viewpoint of both the controller and the respondent, and the other is more important for the controller than for the respondent.

The word "group" is occasionally used to designate an aggregate of persons who share some characteristic or set of characteristics. This kind of group is really better thought of as a grouping, a classification, or a category. The persons included may have no consciousness of belonging, nor any particular interaction with other members. Thus, one speaks of tall men, short men, blonds, and brunettes. A controller can base an appeal on the distinctive characteristic of such a group. These groupings or aggregates are of great practical importance in the sense that any classifying and grouping is important where a large number of variables is involved. They are of no theoretical importance aside from the qualities that characterize the category.

The second way that "group" is used is to refer to the distinctive behavior that arises out of an individual's relations to an aggregate perceived as an object. The individuals in this type of group are distinguished not so much by shared characteristics as by a shared relation to the perceived object. Thus, whereas in the first kind of group the controller would regard doctors as doctors, here he would consider them as individuals influenced by the medical association. The respondent's response acts will be affected and shaped by his orientation to all objects he perceives as relevant. When the word "group" is used to refer to this phenomenon it is more accurate, although still somewhat metaphorical, to speak of a group as an actor.

This second conception of group is needed to explain otherwise inexplicable behavior. For example, doctors pay dues to a medical association, attend meetings, vote for leaders, and so on. Obviously, they do so because of their loyalty to the perceived object, in this case the medical association. Pure group behavior, as distinct from merely summed individual behavior, is most clearly seen in situations in which an individual behaves in a manner we would not expect if he were not orienting to a perceived object. For example, individual trade union members temporarily give up their jobs and withdraw support from their employer in order to secure union recognition. We say it is in part their loyalty to the union that causes them to do this.

In *The Modern Democratic State* [1] the great British political theorist A. D. Lindsay made the point that certain associations, such as the state and the church, have indeterminate purposes. But all groups or associations, when viewed as causing people to do certain things they could not otherwise be expected to do, may be said to have indeterminate purposes. Their purpose is in fact whatever purpose people assign to them. What are some of the political consequences of these groups that become instruments or facilitators?

A respondent may view a group in two related but different ways. He may view it as an object that is essentially facilitative in relation to his personality. He attaches to it as a matter of self-identification. It serves for the individual one of the same functions that physical property performs, namely, it gives him some object of his own. And, of course, all groups that are not his own are those of other persons, and he orients to these as he would to the property of others. Thus, of all the objects that go to make up a person's psychic world, many are groups of the type we are considering here, and these serve to support the personality.

But groups are also used instrumentally—that is, the individual uses a group as an object to increase the effectiveness of his own capacities in certain situations. And, likewise, he see other persons being made more effective by their use of groups. How do these two uses of groups shape and mediate the responses to control acts? We shall consider first the supportive use and second the instrumental use.

Let us see what happens when an individual responds to a control act. At first he interacts in a way that is at least tolerable to his personality system. Next he becomes aware, either consciously or subconsciously, of the intervention of a control act, which calls for a response different from what he and others would ordinarily expect. As we have seen, his response will lie somewhere between automatic compliance and intransigence. In any event, the need for response will create a discomfort, and he will try to make sense out of the control act and to test its consequences in terms of his own personality system. Because a part of his personality system is built around groups for which he has some kind of feeling, his perception of these will affect how he interprets the control act. The more relevant the perception is to the requirements of the control act the greater the involvement will be. Thus, if the control act requires a response that would threaten an object to which he has a strong loyalty, his discomfort will be more acute and he will have a graver problem of personality reorganization. He will be subjected to what are generally called cross-pressures.

The perceived group becomes a kind of a mediator and organizer for the respondent. Although it may reduce the discomfort resulting from a control act, it may also sharpen the discomfort and greatly complicate the problem of finding an ameliorating response.

The various ways in which group attachments affect the control process may be illustrated by taking the case of a city council and the Red Cross. A council passes an ordinance curtailing solicitations of funds, thus limiting those who solicit in the name of the Red Cross. The Red Cross might be thought of as affecting the responses of three classes of people. First, there are those who have a vague protective feeling toward the Red Cross and who believe that its members do good work. They also respect the council and in general are inclined to go along with both. But in this case, to support the council is to injure the Red Cross, and vice versa.

There are also those who do volunteer work on behalf of the Red Cross. Red Cross work helps give meaning to their lives. They are more intimately involved with the fate of the Red Cross but they also have a sense of obligation to the council. How are their responses affected by these attachments?

Finally, there are those who are still more directly related and are clearer beneficiaries of the money raised and the services rendered. These people have a more instrumental view of the Red Cross and see the action of the council as a direct threat. How will their responses to the action of the council be affected by their feeling for the Red Cross?

The foregoing examples are designed to show how groups affect responses to control and how varying kinds and degrees of attachment account for the differences in response. When those individuals who are most intensely attached to the group respond, it is often said that the group itself responds. It is this that usually produces the personification of the group.

A control act that threatens a highly regarded group tends to cause the forging of new ties among those who share the same feelings toward the perceived group. It may even lead to the perceiving of a new group based upon a shared feeling for the old one. This suggests that the process of creating groups is essentially an outgrowth of a demand for a certain integrity and comfort in the personality system. There is something here that is closely akin to the demand for equality, as it was discussed in the previous chapter. The adjustive process tends to be eased if a control act is seen as affecting all groups, or all relevant ones, in somewhat the same way. The persuasional process as a means of control is most concerned with, and most affected by, the existence of groups.

One of the responses an individual can make to a control act is called countercontrol. This is especially relevant to a discussion of groups. Countercontrol takes the form of explicit resistance to control acts. As such it reflects an effort to modify or negate control acts. When a prospective respondent to a control act argues that it adversely affects a group to which he is attached, he is using the group as a weapon or instrument. He may appeal for the welfare of the group toward which the controller also has a strong feeling; or he may try to convince the controller that there is widespread resistance to the control act which might lead to the controller losing the support he will need for other purposes.

In these situations only existing groups would be used. However, since groups can be deliberately created for use as control instruments, it has become possible—indeed common in nonfatalistic politics—to create groups mainly for improving countercontrol. The whole countercontrol process has been revolutionized by this discovery. This indicates the importance of the insight of David Truman, a leading student of groups in politics, that interest groups are groups which are designed to make claims on government and that associations come into existence for the purpose of restoring stability and equilibrium to group relations.[2]

Widespread countercontrol against the traditional control acts is the action component of what many refer to as the rise of democracy. Democracy as a concept, however, shares the same limitations as the concepts of power and authority. None of these suggests action. The importance of countercontrol through the use of both existing and deliberately created groups, however, is suggested by the fact that whenever control trouble exists or is anticipated attempts are always made to reduce countercontrol and especially to dissolve groups that might increase the effectiveness of countercontrol. Hence, in a totalitarian country groups that are widely affected by the people, or by strategic persons, are attacked with a view toward loosening the ties that bind people to them. Furthermore, rigid control is exercised over the creation of new ones. For example, in the Soviet Union there is an attempt to monopolize all nonpolity sentiments by absorbing into feelings for the Communist party all affective feelings that might develop around groups.

It is difficult to outlaw any group as groups. Because a group is basically a mental construct that is loved or hated, the only way of destroying the motivating effect of any group is to brainwash its members, that is, wash out either the perception or the feeling or both.

From the viewpoint of motivation or influence, the psychological factor of groups is their most important aspect. In forming them, the individual organizes and relates his thoughts and feelings. He creates objects of loyalty, entities to which he can cling. He tends in this process to simplify and to attribute to them more unity than actually exists. The perceived group becomes an ideal to be achieved in practice, but it is a kind of indeterminate ideal, a dynamic idea. This is what makes groups seem to have a life of their own.

Every group has a descriptive and an instrumental aspect and these aspects are interdependent. In large measure the effectiveness of a group as an instrument is dependent upon its describable solidarity and unity. And unity in a social formation is dependent upon its effectiveness as an instrument. This means that an individual must be responsive to what for him is outside control in order to gain the benefits of solidarity and effectiveness.

Thus, whether or not a social group results in greater freedom for the individual is always a matter for empirical investigation. It cannot be taken for granted. This notion, however, leads to a consideration of what is meant when a group makes a claim for freedom.

Polemical literature is filled with examples of groups making claims for freedom. The church, the party, the business enterprise, and the nation-state make claims for freedom in substantially the same way individuals do. In fact, most personification of groups is among those who claim freedom from some controller. For example, it is claimed that the nation-state should be free of the control of other nation-states. Because only individual human beings can feel discomfort and exhilaration, no group can make a meaningful and distinctive claim to freedom on this basis. The fundamental basis of a claim for freedom must rest on the desirability of freedom for individual members. Thus a claim for freedom must be essentially a claim for individual freedom. A group's claim is simply the shorthand generalization of the claims of a particular number of persons.

However, as we have seen, every group is also an agency of control and countercontrol and thus it is capable of improvement and deterioration. A particular group is perfected as an instrument of control by refining the interaction pattern that characterizes it and by strengthening and clarifying the perception of it. Refinement comes in large part through continuity of the patterns and the adjustment of them to the constantly changing world in which they exist. A control act that originates outside of a group is always a threat to the continuity and self-adjustment of the group. Thus persons who perceive a pattern and who care about it are cast in the role of resisters to relevant intervening control acts. The persons who perceive most clearly and care most deeply are officers or leaders and they are thus the spearhead of resistance, as well as the ones who make most use of the group as an instrument. Their appeal for freedom in the name of the group is the loudest and the clearest, and they are the ones who have the most to lose from intervening control acts. They argue that the controls they impose on the perceived pattern in the name of the group should have priority over imminent external controls.

This works in reverse too. Rewards made by outside controllers to the name of the group will be distributed disproportionately between leaders and nonleaders. All of this suggests that the claim of a group for freedom is especially a claim for freedom of the coordinators or leaders of the group. We may then ask: Is the claim to freedom more than a claim for freedom on the part of the leadership of the social formation?

There is this much more to be said. The mere identifiable existence of a group is an indication of an extremely complex entity. This is true of it as a perception, where there are slight differences in the entity between perceivers. It is equally true of it as a pattern of acts which are describable by external and detached observers. A group cannot be completely manufactured by human technicians any more than a single human being can be manufactured, and thus it cannot be fully described. A fitting and adjusting process goes on continuously. The mere passage of time assures this. Because these often minute adjustments are made by human beings, the effect of any external control act is not wholly predictable. Thus it is that a claim for freedom on the part of a group is in part a claim for the avoidance of the control act whose delicate and minute adjustments take place pragmatically and piecemeal.

In a sense a group always mediates between a controller and an individual. It does this by trying to maintain a maximum of predictability in a situation where it is practically impossible to ascertain precisely what causes the existing relations, and hence impossible to tell what will create new ones or what their consequences will be. If all of this sounds very conservative it can only be answered that groups reflect a conservative component in behavior, in that they tend to perpetuate existing behavior and to change only when the consequences are highly predictable. Thus we may conclude that the claim of a group for freedom is a claim for a distinctive freedom. It is not known for sure how to compensate the discomfort of the individual that comes from the unsettling of his behavior pattern, because the behavior pattern is essentially unique to the relations between the individual and the demands of the particular group. Thus, although we may say that the claim to freedom of a group is based upon the claim to freedom for the individual, the particular freedom is so inextricably bound up with the particular pattern that it is impossible to disturb the pattern without disturbing the individual. It is a matter of emphasizing the individual indirectly by emphasizing the pattern directly.

The foregoing analysis indicates that the referent of all meaningful claims of freedom is the individual. This suggests that all claims to freedom by groups should be examined critically. The claims that are made are usually made by the leaders and it cannot be taken for granted that they will use the freedom for the benefit of the contributing individuals. In the United States, the Southern white leaders claim freedom for their states so they can control Negroes according to their own standards. They resist outside interference, because they are afraid of the Negro's potential for countercontrol. As has been argued earlier, the avowal and acceptance of resistance and countercontrol is the action component of democracy. It is the most effective single guarantor of freedom.

One of the recent developments in the study of politics has been a shift from concern with legalistic and formalistic approaches, from what is often called the abstract individual, to a study of groups and group conflict.[3] In the light of the above discussion, what does the phrase "group conflict" mean, and what are the prospects of a study of politics based upon groups rather than upon individuals?

Basically, of course, group conflict simply means patterned conflict in which the conflicting human actors are viewed as responding to the demands, propensities, and predispositions which are attributed to groups. It also means those conflicts in which the actors use the perception of the group as an instrument. Most group conflicts are actually conflicts among leaders of different groups. As such, they are strengthened by their capacity for manipulating the perception, and conflict that uses better instruments is apt to be more intense. But the effectiveness of the instrument depends upon the existence of a pattern, and such increased effectiveness as the instrument contributes is in part at least offset by the greater systematicness and depersonalization of the conflict that is imposed. Group conflict is, in short, organized conflict but nevertheless the conflict of individuals.

What the group theory of politics really amounts to is a recognition that there are other important patterns or groups than those legally and constitutionally adopted. To speak of group conflict as the main course of politics is to shift the perspective in a necessary direction. But it is only a shift in perspective; the important thing is what happens. What the group emphasis is intended to do is wholly sound; that is, to shift attention to behavior *patterns,* regardless of what they are called and regardless of how they are personified.

Until the development of sociology and social psychology, the main thinking about the nature of groups came from the field of jurisprudence. Groups have always been a source of great difficulty for the law. The law deals with control of individuals on the basis of discrete acts, and in so far as a group results from discrete acts it presents no particular problem. But the law has had great difficulty in getting at groups as instruments. How to get behind individual behavior to the causes of that behavior and its exceptional vigor in many instances confronted the law with a problem that it has not yet solved. Thus, all the argument about the rights of corporations and guilt by association continue unabated.

Today some groups are ignored by the law. This means that the individual who contributes to a pattern and uses it as an instrument is treated simply as an individual. Other groups are recognized and regulated, which usually means that the leaders are subjected to special legal powers and disabilities. Still other groups, such as corporations and government agencies, are treated as creations of the law. Here the law, as a control instrument, prescribes some of the patterns of relations and places the weight of the law behind those seeking compliance with them. But since the most unique quality of a group is based on images in men's minds which influence their behavior, the law has great difficulty regulating the images. The attempt to outlaw the Communist Party in the United States is an example of the problem presented here.

The study of politics has always been filled with discussions of social classes and class systems. The writings of Karl Marx have done a great deal to intensify this concern with classes. How do they fit into the picture sketched here? Our concept of group is designed to be used in a broad enough sense to cover the class phenomenon. A class may be simply a characterization of uniformities in behavior, and as such it presents no special problem. But a new dimension is added when there is class consciousness. We must then think in terms of the special qualities of class perceptions.

When men behave in a certain way because they perceive themselves as members of a class, or when they view the behavior of others as class-determined behavior, the class becomes an influencing object. Although Marx did not discover classes, he made everyone class-conscious and thus emphasized class-determined behavior. He and his followers forged instruments out of what others had discovered long before. Whether a class is an instrument of deliberate control depends upon the particular class and upon the exploitation of class consciousness. This can only be determined by empirical investigation. The universality and persistence of classes is better explained by a consideration of those phenomena around which groups seem universally to grow than it is by a consideration of the distinctive *form* of class.

In bringing this discussion of groups to a close, let us turn specifically to the field of politics. We have come to recognize three forms of democracy in recent times, which can be differentiated by the controller's attitude toward groups. The three are Jacobin democracy, totalitarian democracy, and pluralistic democracy.

Jacobin democracy tries to eliminate what it conceives as the special resisting quality of mediating social formations between individual respondents and the main controllers. Thus, Jacobin democracy attempts to dissolve or neutralize politically the mediating formations, just as socialism's purpose is to neutralize attachment to private property. Totalitarian democracy, which shares many of the characteristics of Jacobin democracy, attempts to use the existing groups in order to strengthen its controls. If it cannot use them, it tries to dissolve or neutralize them because they impede control. Pluralistic democracy regards control as emanating from the groups acting as agencies, and it views the central and more remote control system as an instrument to perfect the controls of the many groups. The main perspective of pluralistic democracy is that of facilitating countercontrol.

The special role of groups in the political process should be fairly clear by now. The perspective of politics is that of controlling the more remote environment in a deliberate or calculated fashion. The more remote the control act is from the response act, the greater the need for intervening formations, both as mediators and as instruments of countercontrol. The controller exercises control in the more remote environment only through a chain or a set of agencies. The individual responds to the impact of the control acts mainly as a contributor to a chain or set of groups. Hence, he responds to the control acts mainly in terms of ongoing patterns that he is striving to round out or to fulfill.

Samuel Lubell, in his perceptive work *The Revolt of the Moderates*,[4] takes note of the almost exclusive concern of American politics with foreign policy, economic policy, and what he calls racial-ethnic and religious matters. If these concerns are translated into concern with other polities, with economic matters, and with religious matters, they constitute the most enduring concern of politics over the course of human history.

12

Religion and Polity

A distinction between politics and religion appears to be universal, but equally universal is the interpenetration of the two. Religion manifests itself in sets of beliefs, in practices, and in groups, just as politics does. Although religious beliefs, practices, and groups are different from their political counterparts, they are related to each other. From the perspective of politics, religion is a problem, and from the perspective of religion, politics is a problem. Thus, a theory of politics must explain this enduring distinctiveness and the equally enduring relatedness.

An empirical political system arises from man's universal concern with his more remote environment, whereas religious systems arise out of man's concern with the ultimate and the timeless, or what will be called here the *most* remote environment, as distinguished from the *more* remote environment. This accounts for the distinctiveness between politics and religion. However, because individuals are characterized by a certain continuity and integrity, man's concerns with the more remote and the most remote environments are related. This leads us to expect that each individual would tend to reconcile the two, and that this would be reflected in social systems.

Because of the adjacency of the two it is possible to define religion in terms of politics. Thus we can define religion as those allowable beliefs, practices, and groups which express man's concern with ultimate matters. The word "allowability" does not mean that politics should determine the allowability of religion, or that it always does. It simply stresses that, viewed as relevant to politics and the control problem which produces it, any political system will have norms setting allowable limits to religious beliefs, practices, and groups.

Religion has been defined by the theologian Paul Tillich as that which is concerned with the ultimate. Jacques Maritain, the leading lay philosopher of the Catholic Church, says: "The human person is ordained directly to God as its absolute ultimate end. Its direct ordination to God transcends every created common good—both the common good of the political society and the intrinsic common good of the universe." [1]

Reinhold Niebuhr, speaking of the religious concern, says: "There must always be a religious element in the hope of a just society. Without the ultrarational hopes and passions of religion no society will ever have the courage to conquer despair and attempt the impossible; for the vision of a just society is an impossible one, which can be approximated only by those who do not regard it as impossible." [2]

H. M. Kallen, in an article entitled "Democracy's True Religion," discoursed on the nature of religious belief, from the viewpoint of a secular philosopher:

> Belief is religious when the believer asserts—regardless of their absence from all actual experience and vision—"the sub-

stance of things hoped for, and the evidence of things not seen." However valid and compelling the alternatives to the divine object of belief may seem to others, however reason and perception may require its appraisal as an untrue illusion, it remains to the man who honestly and sincerely believes supremely real, unchallengeably true. For him the alternative other Gods are the errors and illusions. Not uncommonly the measure of his faith in the divine being of his choice is the depth of his animosity toward its competitors and the energy of his endeavor to destroy their competitive powers.[3]

The strength and endurance of the religious tie have often been noted. Joachim Wach, in his *Sociology of Religion,* says "worship with all it implies is not only an additional bond but very probably the most important non-biological tie between people."[4] Alfred Bertholet, writing in the Encyclopedia of the Social Sciences, also comments on this aspect: "The bond which united the adherents of cult is stronger than that of any other tie except that of blood."[5]

Given the nature of politics and religion as described here, what can we expect about boundary controversies and the particular respects in which politics and religion mutually support each other?

Politically, religion is usually regarded as an intrusion in the affairs of the here and now. Religious beliefs may be used instrumentally to serve the ends of the immediate world, but even then its appeal is based on notions or beliefs about the ultimate. Man's concern is with an environment beyond his experience, and he does not tend to see that environment as pure process. Moreover, he tends to see that environment as orderly, and as one to which he must adjust rather than control. Thus it is that the more remote environment is closely related to the most remote environment. There is also a strong adjustive or adaptive propensity in the religious perspective. Religion deals with the absolute in life. But the very act of conceiving an absolute draws with it a perception of the nature of the absolute. And since this absolute cannot be known through the senses or through reason, individuals are bound to have different ideas about it, based to some extent on their own experience. This is why men disagree about the nature of God and what God requires of man. Because ordinary scientific inquiry cannot be applied to religion, individuals do not want to subject their belief in the absolute to the tests of scientific proof.

When one perceives the existence of something he gives it a particular form and tends to personify it. The less personal experience he has with it, the more this perception supports his subjective belief. Fundamentally this explains a great deal of the kinship between religion and politics. Man can experience the perceived unit of his more remote environment only in a limited sense, and he cannot experience the whole nature of the absolute. He must fill in with his imagination. And his imagination is based on his experience.

What we have been saying here is that once man perceives a wider environment and becomes involved in affairs beyond the range of his personal experience, he gives form and quality to that of which he becomes conscious. The organization of his psyche concerning his more remote environment is based on his own experience and is supplemented by the experience of others who communicate their experience to him, mainly through the culture. However, in the case of the most remote and absolute environment, none of his perception is based directly and absolutely on his own or others' ordinary sense experience.

It would be strange indeed if man could draw a sharp boundary line between his perception of the more remote and the most remote environments. The line between the close at hand and the more remote is wide and shaded, and the same is true of the line between the more and most remote. There may well be as much objective reality about God and heaven as there is about a nation-state. But in the minds of men, the perception of one merges with and overlaps the perception of the other.

As man perceives units of his remote environment he develops affective feelings for what he perceives. Differentiation is inherent in the process of perceiving, and so some objects will repel him and others will attract him. This is an integral part of the organizing process.

We have already seen that a great deal of so-called political action is taken on faith, and responded to as a matter of faith. More of religious action is based upon faith. What happens when two objects of faith seem to require different and even contradictory acts? If the love of one object must be sacrificed for the demands of another, which one is sacrificed? This is the kind of problem that grows out of the fundamental relation between religion and politics. Man will search desperately to avoid the direct confrontation and will try to reconcile the two. But when they cannot be reconciled, the secular or political tends to prevail, mainly because it is more firmly based on sense impressions and concrete fact. It is significant, though, that the political rarely prevails without being modified by the religious attachment.

Both religion and politics are the outgrowth of man's perception of that which he does not fully experience. What he perceives but does not experience sensually to any appreciable degree produces religion. What he experiences partially and strategically produces politics.

No discussion of religion and politics is complete without some mention of what is generally called the institutionalization of religion, the practices and groups with substantial continuity and longevity. The institutionalization of religion is a direct outgrowth of the nature of religion, or the religious experience. It is the sharing of religious experience and the drive to find understandable and shareable meaning in it that produce religious institutions. Thus, man tends to personify God or the gods as actors, and to refer to the operation of the absolute in earthly terms. Phrases like King of Kings, Kingdom of God, and City of God are examples of the need to give form to the unknowable.

On the basis of what has been said above, one would expect a combining of religious and political institutions, as in a theocracy, or at least a basic similarity between religious and political institutions. In the face of all the similarities, however, some basic differences should appear. Religion is even more heavily endowed with ritual and ceremony than politics is. Why is this so? Ritual emerges from efforts to make tangible the faith element in a relationship. Or it may emerge as a hypothesized causal agency. It develops where there is faith in the existence of a causal and orderly relationship but where the causal relationship cannot be demonstrated. Faith must be sustained in religion just as in politics. The main difference is that in religious faith, all-important and certain knowledge about the consequences of causal acts is relatively unknown. Thus, the ritualistic element in religion is always greater than in politics.

Another difference between religion and politics stems from the fact that politics is based upon the notion that man can exercise some control over what happens beyond his immediate environment. Thus, the perspective of politics is control by calculation or deliberation. The world of politics is one of becoming rather than of being. Religion, on the other hand, is not subject to human modification; it is an absolute world. The perspective of religion is self-adjustment—that is, adjusting to the requirements of the absolute. The perspective of politics is control of others, and finding out what control requires.

Much of politics is concerned with the so-called conflict between the more and most remote environments and the close-at-hand and more remote. The former is intensified by separate institutionalization of the two realms, which leads to conflicts between church and state, clericalism and secularism. Religious norms, agents, and agencies come into conflict with those of politics. But it should not be supposed that abolishing or fusing the two sets of agents and agencies would eliminate the conflict: even in theocracies, the rulers have schismatic quarrels about true doctrine. In fact, some order is provided by the separate institutions of politics and religion. Religion without clerics is unthinkable, Kallen notwithstanding. Church and state are specializations that develop out of the concerns and needs of human beings. To perceive a religious realm is to create a church. To perceive a more remote environment is to create a polity.

At the beginning of this chapter we cited a few quotations to the effect that next to the blood tie, the religious tie is the strongest of all human ties. How is this to be explained? The blood tie grows out of the closest and most knowable relation of man. It represents the world he knows best through actual experience, and it is the referent for all other relations and all other ties. That man should cling most steadfastly to that which he knows and experiences most intimately is easy to understand.

But if the strength of the blood tie needs no special explanation, can we say the same about the religious tie? Man feels insignificant when he contemplates the infinite number of other persons in the world, and when he contemplates eternity. He also sees, at least dimly, the insignificance of the few people around him—his family, neighbors, and friends. He understands that if he regards himself as anything but an accidental eruption of natural forces, then he must regard every other man as having meaning. Thus, strong ties are forged between men around notions of the nature of ultimate reality.

What an individual claims for himself in terms of ultimate

reality he must also claim for others, and it is this concern with the ultimate that characterizes the religious tie. It explains at once the strength of the tie and the intense bitterness that can develop out of different concepts of the nature of ultimate reality. The knowledge that gives strength to the blood tie is matched by the demand for knowability in the essentially unknowable religious realm. The religious tie is man's tie to the human species. In between the tie based upon the most knowable and the least knowable there is a world of flux and change, a world of becoming which tends to be somewhat more malleable and tentative because the mixture of what is knowable and what is not makes it less clear.

Religious agents recognize the vital relation between the close at hand and the most remote environment. Hence there is emphasis upon the importance, integrity, and independence of the family unit, as compared with other control agents and agencies. The controversy over the control of education is an outgrowth of the essential nature of religion and politics and should be expected, if the nature of religious tie and the blood tie is properly understood.

13

Economy and Polity

From the perspective of the politician, the economy and economic activity present both a problem and a source of support. Like religion, economics is universally differentiated from politics, but the two are interrelated and interpenetrate each other.

Obviously, man is not only concerned with the most remote and more remote environments. He is also involved in the more directly and immediately perceived environment. This is composed of daily, ongoing needs and problems. In his immediate environment an individual has close-at-hand relationships with other people and is involved in closely meshed activities. It is man's participation in this everyday world that anchors him to the more remote and most remote worlds. His more direct and proximate concerns give rise to a class of beliefs, practices, and groups which we call economic, and which, as a system, constitute an economy.

From the perspective of political theory, economic activities are those allowed to man for the direct purpose of serving his own more immediate and personal needs. Politics arises out of intermediate-range needs and concerns, religion out of ultimate concerns, and economics out of particularistic concerns.

It must be emphasized that this is not meant to be an absolute definition of economics, but rather a description from the viewpoint of politics. The "allowable" aspect is again stressed, not in descriptive terms but in terms of the norms of politics. The reasons for the differentiation and the relatedness between politics and economics are the same as for religion and politics. Economic systems grow out of the interplay between man's particularistic concerns and his more and most remote concerns. This distinction, barely apparent in the life of an individual, becomes very obvious in social life—that is, in group activity and in shared beliefs and practices.

The distinction made here between the economy and the polity is not unlike the one made by Aristotle in *Politics*. He distinguishes between the affairs of the household and the affairs of the polity. It is also worth noting that our word "economy" derives from the Greek word for household.

In any polity there is a distinction between approved self-seeking behavior and disapproved, or even prohibited, self-seeking behavior. Whether a particular kind of activity is approved or disapproved depends, of course, on the polity in question. *An economic act is one in which providing directly for oneself and members of one's own immediate environment is approved and encouraged.* Thus, in a society in which lending money for interest is forbidden, lending is not an economic activity. In the United States the carrying and delivering of mail is not an economic activity, although the items carried by express companies produce economic activity. Where every act can be done with the avowed purpose of serving the more immediate needs of self and family, economic life is commensurate with life itself. Where no act for self and family is approved, there is no economy, no economic life. There is wholly a political and religious life. Where no self-regarding act is forbidden, we say anarchy prevails; where no self-regarding act is approved, we speak of a totalitarian system or situation.

Economics, then, has to do with the serving of the more immediate environment, including the self. But since man always has a more remote environment which makes demands on him, the substance of economic activities is not naturally determined. In one society an act may be economic, in another it may be political, and in still another it may be religious. It is the perspective in which acts are undertaken and approved or disapproved that determines their character. In any society, the almost purely economic acts—there are no absolutely pure ones—are those performed with the avowed purpose of improving an individual's own condition and that of his household without social or political disapproval. On the periphery of the economy are those activities about which there is indecision or controversy as to whether or not they should be approved for personal gain. Noneconomic acts are those explicitly forbidden for personal gain. Thus, the definition of the economy as those acts undertaken for profit comes close to providing a useful and realistic conception of the economy.

Does this mean, we may ask, that an act undertaken for aesthetic satisfaction, such as joining a neighborhood art club, is an economic act? Is it properly considered an economic activity? Presumably people join such clubs for aesthetic and self-improvement reasons, and the activity is not frowned upon even though it is self-regarding. To the extent that the act is approved self-seeking it is economic. However, to deal with our kind of world we have had to concentrate upon measurable phenomena—hence the concentration upon physical material and the medium of exchange or money in the economy. If an individual gets paid for going to a meeting of an art club, or if he sells a picture he produces as a result of his participation in the club, no one doubts that it is an economic activity. But when he pursues his own satisfactions for psychological or intangible compensation, his behavior is really no different, at least from the perspective of politics.

Many persons distinguish those acts undertaken for intangible and unmeasurable satisfaction from the economic by calling them cultural and giving them especially strong social encouragement. For example, Robert MacIver, a leading contemporary political theorist, argues for political intervention in the economy but for political withdrawal from the cultural. This is essentially a pragmatic policy argument about what people should be allowed to do for themselves. It should be pointed out, however, that the sharp distinction drawn in recent years between acts undertaken for tangible and measurable return and those undertaken for intangible and unmeasurable return is a distortion of human motivation. It is now perfectly clear that acts undertaken for tangible and measurable return are also perfectly capable of yielding an increment of intangible and nonmeasurable return. A people's culture is the product of what they do in toto.

Most people spend a good deal of their time looking after the needs and desires of themselves and their family. Since most societies approve many activities for this purpose, economic activities constitute a large part of the life of any person. Satisfactions and pains in life are experienced personally and intimately. It is little wonder then that people tend to view the more remote and the most remote world in the perspective of their own needs and desires. It is also little wonder that it takes so much political and religious effort to get people to forego a clear and direct personal satisfaction in order to gain a vague and problematical satisfaction.

The perspective of control is still a valid one for viewing

the immediate world or environment. What happens when man undertakes to control his immediate environment and the ongoing social pattern cooperates with him? In the first place, he organizes this environment into units toward which he develops feelings of attachment. The main perceived unit has always been the family, but in recent times the firm or enterprise has come to perform some of the functions once performed by the family. The basic process of unit recognition and perception in the immediate world is not substantially different from that through which man organizes his more remote environment. Nor is the essential nature of the control methods different. As has already been indicated, the particular form of the methods and the distribution of usage among the methods vary. But this is a difference of degree and not of kind. Each perceived unit has its aspects of resultant and instrument, and any unit also may be regarded as either an agent or agency. With the passage of time and the development of awareness, the units have been more sharply bounded. The family, which once shaded off into various degrees of remote blood relationship, is now, in most Western societies, sharply defined and somewhat legally and formally bounded. The same is true of the firm or enterprise. Contributors to a firm are approved in contributing only to the degree that they serve their own needs, always, of course, within the limit specified by the controllers of the more remote environment and the imperatives of the prevailing religious system.

There are two concepts that are universally associated with economics, and some discussion of these should be helpful in exploring the fundamental relation between the economic and the noneconomic realms of life. These concepts are property and profit.

The term property is often modified by the word "private." Property is usually taken to be something that someone holds or possesses. Private property is something that a nonofficial person holds. The idea that a person holds something often leads to the idea that that which is held is the property. Actually, however, property is anything that cannot be rightfully taken away or denied to a person except by highly specialized methods and for generally convincing reasons. Property is that which man can hold and control against the rest of the world with the aid of a portion of the rest of the world. Thus to insist upon holding and controlling property is to insist that one be left unmolested for exercising a proprietorship over it. Property is characterized by the way it is protected against others, not by what it is or by who holds it. It is a product of letting men seek their own ends.

Property in any society—and the concept of it varies greatly —is consciously determined by the controllers of the more remote environment, and unconsciously determined by usage and tradition. No man can control his immediate environment without instruments appropriate to that control. The permissiveness of certain instruments is based in practice upon types of control in the more remote environment. Far from being a natural right, property is in many ways the least natural of phenomena. Man cannot take for his own use whatever he needs. The natural claim is denied by the very concept of property. If one has a general moral right to look out for oneself and one's own, then there are specific rights or properties which are necessary for the fulfillment of the more general right. But to make the property of the natural holder secure, it is necessary to impose an unnatural restraint upon others who covet the holding. That property should be regarded as the touchstone of the economic realm seems perfectly clear. That property law and family law should be intimately related needs no explanation. That so much of the discussion of the relation between the economy and the political should turn around notions of property is readily explained when we see property arguments as essentially arguments about what a man should be allowed to do for himself with social and political approval.

Profit, broadly defined, is simply the added increment of satisfaction that one gets back over and above what he contributes to an activity. A profitable act is one in which satisfaction outweighs discomfort or deprivation. The profit motive, then, is simply the motive to look out for and improve oneself and one's family.

The profit concept came into sharper focus with the development of a money and industrial economy. Money makes it possible to measure the value of acts, and thus to make closer calculations of the balance between input and output. The profit approach has now been formalized and explicitly used to motivate men to do many things. It has always been a potent motivating force, but by being formalized it has been more widely used as a control motivator by those concerned with both the more remote environment and the immediate environment. To a degree, the emphasis upon profit has replaced the emphasis upon property. Fundamentally, however, they are both responses to the same demand. The reason a person wants property is that as an instrument it enables him to make a profit and improve himself, or at least sustain existence. To describe in a society the permissible profitmaking, and the processes that are entailed, is to describe the economy of a people.

In our own time, economic systems, the systems of approved self-serving, are essentially national economic systems. What is approved self-serving, and the traditional and deliberate regulations imposed on self-serving, varies with the contemporary form of the polity, the nation-states. But like all political systems, all economic systems have certain elements in common, because economic systems are an outgrowth of certain basic human needs and demands. The development of a given economic system is also conditioned by traditions and deliberate regulations, and different traditions and different deliberate regulations bring about essential modifications in economic systems. Viewing the development of economic systems both historically and comparatively it is possible to discern certain classes of economic systems. The classes used in this discussion characterize economic systems as primitive, mercantile, and industrial. Every existing economic system has elements of each, and at the present time, economic systems may be found in the world which contain each of the three. A primitive economy is essentially an economy with a low differentiation, a mercantile economy emphasizes trade and distribution, and in industrial economy emphasizes fabrication.

There are three kinds of primitive economies: the hunting economy, the agrarian and raw materials economy, and feudalism, a transitional economy. In the first one, economic activity is dominated by the requirements of the hunt. Religion, politics, and art are affected and reflect the economy. Life is nomadic; there is only minimal division of labor. Exchange plays a less important role and operates within narrow limits, usually of the family or clan. There is always great pressure to survive physically, and economic activities seem to consist mainly of fulfilling physical needs. The processing of material things in order to make them more useful for human consumption is minimal and largely undifferentiated. Wars between polities tend to arise over hunting grounds and to be intensified by cultural differences.

The agrarian and raw materials economy represents a more positive effort by man to exercise control over nature. Plants are cultivated, minerals mined, and animals domesticated. This requires the people to be somewhat fixed geographically. The processing is still simple and the division of labor is minimal. The satisfaction of material needs gives color to the whole system. But this kind of society is capable of great complexity and division of labor. The most respected self-seeking activity is the extraction of raw material from the earth, either by mining or by cultivation, and a whole social structure may be built upon the varying degrees of respectability that emerge. A plantation system based upon human slavery is probably the most complicated development of an agrarian and raw materials economic system.

Feudalism is a third or transitional type of primitive economic system. The essence of feudalism as an economic-social-political system is a complex interaction pattern built around the simple relation of man to the soil. In the feudal society a man's attachment to a specific unit of soil is so pervasive that a polity is only dimly perceived and arouses weak feelings. Self-seeking predominates in a fundamental sense but it is rigidly regulated by many specific traditional controls, as opposed to general and deliberate controls.

Feudalism develops where there is no strong attachment to a polity which transcends the attachment to the soil. The extent to which real property law still reflects much of the feudal relationship indicates clearly what its main base was. If the position is taken that the fundamental relation in society is that between man and a plot of ground then the absence of any countervailing ties or relation results in feudalism. Once a more general attachment—that is, an attachment based upon a more varied relationship—is felt, the tie to the soil becomes only one of a number of ties. As loyalty to king and country grew stronger, it superseded some of the relationships based on the soil. Rights in land came to take their place alongside other rights instead of being the source of all rights. Some of the things that had been approved self-seeking, and economic in nature, came to be approved only for public purposes and became noneconomic. For example, private armies gave way to armies of the king.

All primitive economies are essentially adjustive. We might

say that life is dominated by economics rather than by politics or religion. It is always easy in a primitive economic system to show how the art, the political institutions, and the religious practices are related to the basic task of sustaining existence.

The mercantile economy emphasizes trade and distribution. Except for simple and primitive barter, trade is a complicated affair. Barter suffices for trade among families and neighbors, but trade with people one does not know requires a more sophisticated system. In the first place, emphasis upon trade represents a movement away from the purely adjustive approach. It reflects a belief that the randomness and hostility in the environment can be reduced by positive action. A life based upon an agrarian and raw materials exploitation is limited by what can be grown and what can be mined, but through trade people are able to cooperate for the purpose of satisfying a greater variety of wants. However, trade demands more than the will to go beyond mere adjustment; it requires dealing with people one does not know and a concern with the more remote environment. Such symbols as money, weights and measures, and eventually credit and a common system of law (norms) become matters of great concern once the notion of trade takes hold.

In short, concern with trade produces a concern with the more remote environment, and the more extensive the trade the more far reaching is the concern with remote environments and environmental factors. It is no accident that political elaboration and sophistication came first among the people who became traders. The notion that ownership is rigid and unchanging, as in the feudal economy, gave way in the trading economy to the idea of property or ownership as something dynamic and fluid. This tends to reduce the traditional element in the regulation of property relations and to produce deliberate changes in the rules that regulate exchange and ownership.

It is no accident that trading people sharpened the perception of the polity, and that nationalism and the rise of the legally bounded nation-states emerged with trade. As long as people's concerns are essentially local and adjustive, they view the more remote world vaguely and imprecisely; not until they perceive the outside world in units are they likely to sharpen their perception of the unit of which they are a part. An ever-expanding trade changes all this. Trading people are inclined to clarify the image of their own polities at the same time as they sharpen up their perceptions of other units. They begin to notice cultural differences. Their concern with the rules that others follow creates a greater concern with their own rules. Only in this way can they have enough understanding to engage in trade. Both traders and nontraders in a polity begin to view trade not only as a means of self-serving but also as a means of perfecting the polity to which they have formed an attachment and an affective feeling. Thus they begin to manipulate trade rules, which inevitably leads to manipulation of subsidies, tariffs, and money.

Mercantilism is what follows when men get the idea that the satisfaction of their infinite needs and desires can be met more adequately by trade. And thus there develops a new class of approved and encouraged self-seeking activities. But this requires a new approach to controlling the more remote environment, and there is not only a change in political perspectives but also a great increase in the amount of political activity. This means the elimination of some approved self-seeking activities and an increase in the activities that are disapproved for self-serving purposes. Common or public regulation measures and standards develop and the rigging of them for private gain is forbidden.

The rise of industrial economies reflects a belief that, by deliberate will, man can diversify still further the satisfaction of his infinite desires, especially his material ones. Instead of relying upon the products of the earth with a minimum of processing and trade, he maximizes diversity through fabrication. Maximizing of trade and processing produces the modern industrial economy which today dominates the economies of the world. This kind of economy is dependent upon the development of new techniques for processing and for widespread cooperation in self-seeking activities. It has also produced startling advances in technology and in division of labor. This has called for a whole rethinking of the allowable self-seeking activities, and throughout the world people are presently engaged in a debate that reflects this rethinking.

In addition to the development of technology and belief in deliberate control in self-seeking, the main requirements of industrialization are human mobility and capital accumulation. Industrialization calls for drastic changes in people's occupations and style of living. This has involved all of the available control methods, with proof and persuasion playing a greater part where industrialization came relatively early and without undue pressure from other polities. In places where industrialization has come later and under pressure, coercion has played a more prominent role.

The dominant form of approved self-seeking used in the industrialized economy has been wages. The acceptance of this form of self-seeking has been steady and widespread, although it met a large measure of resistance in the social structure, where prestige in greater amount has tended to attach to more traditional methods of approved self-serving, such as ownership of and return from land. But differences were recognized and reflected in such distinctions as that between wages, salaries, and fees. And social structures have adapted to the new needs.

Capital accumulation is also necessary for industrialization and has presented in some ways more problems than has the requirement of human mobility. An industrial economy requires special attention to capital accumulation because it must have a great deal of equipment in the form of machinery and special housing. If persons are wholly occupied in producing what they need immediately, they have no time to produce equipment that does not directly satisfy their immediate needs. People must be convinced to forego present consumption in order to produce more in the long run. And not only is there a problem of accumulating capital, but there is also the problem of capital mobility, which will permit the savings in one field to be used for capital development in another. As long as lending money for interest was an unapproved means of self-serving it was not possible to pay for the use of savings. With this method approved and encouraged it was possible to get people to save and lend in order to accumulate the capital necessary for industrialization.

In countries that industrialized earlier, proof and persuasion were the predominant means of effecting capital accumulation. In newer industrial economies coercion has played a more prominent role. Taxation has been more widely used to require people to forego present consumption in order to accumulate capital. To facilitate capital accumulation corporations were invented under which liability for losses was reduced and limited, in order to reduce the risk of self-seeking and enterprising. Moreover, individual accumulators were treated as property owners and a wide range of self-seeking uses of accumulated capital were approved.

The demand that those who were instrumental in accumulating capital should be given free rein in deciding what they should produce for profit—that is, for compensation for foregoing immediate consumption—resulted in the rationalization called *laissez-faire* capitalism. The gist of this rationalization was that if widespread self-seeking in the uses of capital was approved the true needs of the people and of the polity would be unintentionally but most effectively served. Many of the controls that grew out of the needs of an agrarian–raw-materials and mercantile economy were inappropriate for an industrial economy, and the adjustment process was in many cases a long and difficult one. *Laissez-faire* rationalizations were but one manifestation of the process.

The requirements of human mobility and capital accumulation wrought many changes in the general control scheme for the polities in which industrial economic systems developed. They led to the enforcement of credit regulations, control of the value of money, regulation of interest rates, and the development of corporate ownership and delegated control. The deliberate use of general control methods in order to regulate self-seeking, which had begun in the trading economies, was used ever more extensively and subtly in the new industrial economies. The new class of owners, the capitalists, pressed for rules that would help their efforts, and gradually the wage earners caught the idea and asked for deliberate control help in seeking their own ends.

It is not sufficiently realized how much deliberate control there must be in a polity for even a modest industrial economy to function. One might say that an industrial economy is largely a deliberately created system of self-serving, and that it must operate throughout a more remote environment. In this sense, an industrial economy is the model political economy despite the temporary aberrations of the *laissez-faire* apologists who made the mistake of regarding it as a natural economy and therefore one that had to be adjusted to rather than controlled. Both Karl Marx and Adam Smith made the same mistake, even though they both contributed invaluable insights.

Essentially there are two kinds of industrial economies, and they are distinguished by the methods for accumulation of capital and the relations that grow out of these methods. In what is generally called a capitalist industrial economy, capital accumulation is regarded as a self-seeking activity. To this end, a great deal of prestige is vested in the accumulators and they are encouraged and given control over the uses of the capital. In the other type, generally called socialist, capital accumulation is frowned upon or forbidden as a self-seeking activity. Instead of regarding capital accumulation as a legitimate self-seeking act, it is turned into a public or nonself-seeking act by converting savings into taxes. Direct control is placed in the hands of others than those who make the contribution. In fact, a different scheme of control develops which adopts wage and salary paying as the central self-seeking form of action. The profit-seeking motive is not eliminated; only the form of it is changed and made more uniform, and incidentally subject to more deliberate regulation.

No economy, of course, is wholly capitalist or wholly socialist. That is, no economy wholly rejects individual, voluntary saving and enterprising, and no society relies entirely upon its members doing as they will with their capital. Most industrial economies are a combination of the two. Marx argued for the unimpeded self-serving of the wage earner. He thought this would fatalistically produce a utopia without anyone intending it. The advocates of *laissez faire* argued for the unimpeded self-serving of capital accumulators, and thought this could produce a utopia as a by-product. Each believed that a limited type of control should be exercised over the more remote environment, but in effect each denied his own premises by denying that such control could be deliberately used for other purposes. There is no inherent inability to control self-seeking in one area and inherent ability to control it in another. What is desirable self-seeking is always determined by human aspirations and the appropriate relating of ends and means. The most certain thing is that the requirements of an industrial economy are such that the more remote environment must be deliberately controlled, and within a perceived unit. For this reason any industrial economy is a political economy, just as any primitive economy is essentially an economic polity. In an industrial society no one has a natural right to anything; that is, no one is naturally related to anything as the hunter is related to the buffalo by his direct need for meat and clothing.

The critical points in the relation between economics and politics have to do with money and property. This is true whether the form of industrialism is capitalistic or socialistic. Money is the common value denominator of all activities within a greater society. It serves as the standard to which all measurable values are referred. Self-seeking activities designed to modify the value of money per se are almost universally frowned upon and generally forbidden. Thus, controlling the value of money as a standard is a political act par excellence. It is economically relevant but it is an uneconomic act, regardless of how carefully its deliberate aspect is concealed. It is always undertaken for purposes of controlling the more remote environment and not for self-seeking purposes. Or if it is regulated for self-seeking purposes, it is disguised as a regulation in the interests of the polity as a whole. The economic history of all but primitive economies is a history of conflict over the value of money. These are political conflicts because in order to affect the value of money it is necessary to capture control of the political system. One of the main methods by which economic activities are controlled and economies regulated is the deliberate control of the money system. These regulations may take a variety of forms, from declaring what is legal tender to the regulation of credit and interest on capital accumulation.

The concept of property also provides a critical point around which the fundamental relations between economics and politics develop. As we have seen, property is a protected right. It is that which an individual may use in serving his own ends and for which he may receive positive protection. Changes in property are changes in the protection of different instruments for self-serving purposes. The deliberate controller of the more remote environment has the final say about what shall be regarded as property and what shall be protected as property. Every proposed change in the nature and uses of property produces a political debate, the nature of which is not concealed by talk of natural property. The manipulation of what shall be protected as property is never regarded as an approved act for self-serving purposes. This is to be publicly determined, either by deliberate and formal determination or by tacit approval in the form of indifference.

Along with so-called monetary controls, property controls are the other main way in which economic activities are controlled. Property controls are often referred to as direct controls, as distinguished from indirect monetary controls. And once it is conceded that in modern industrial economies political control is dominant, much of the argument about controls revolves around discussions of direct versus monetary controls. Most industrial societies use a combination of the two so the proportion of each is a matter of policy. To tell a manufacturer how much to produce is a direct or property control. To regulate the value of the money with which he is paid, and with which he pays, is an indirect way of accomplishing a similar end.

An important feature of highly developed industrial societies is the large corporation. Is this an economic or a political enterprise? If the polity in which it exists is capitalistic, it is economic. If the polity is socialistic, it is political. But these are largely formalistic distinctions. In both types of big corporations, the main way in which people are allowed to serve their own interests is the same: by wages and salaries. In this sense, and considered only as payers of salaries and wages, they are both economic enterprises. If the ultimate control is also regarded as a legitimate self-seeking activity, then the rest of the firm is an economic enterprise. If ultimate control is regarded as being disapproved for self-seeking ends we are likely to say that it is a political agency. The truth is, however, that formal and explicit control may be approved for self-seeking, but when we watch the regulations that are imposed and the way the self-seeking is limited, we may well conclude that the political is in fact dominant. If formalities are discounted, it will be seen that most large firms are mainly political instrumentalities.

14

Polity and Polity

C. L. Sulzberger, writing in the *New York Times* of May 5, 1956, suggests a parallel between the rise of the Delian League in Greece and the North Atlantic Treaty Organization. He points out that the Delian League rose in the face of a common danger to the various Greek city-states, and that the League fell apart when the danger faded. The main point of his commentary was that just such a fading "perception of danger" was going on within the NATO countries. With the new Soviet line designed to ease tensions, people in member countries were beginning to ask, "What difference does a division more or less really make?"

In 1956 Barbara Ward asked of the leading NATO countries, "Is Our Reappraisal Agonizing Enough?" [1] Her general answer is No. She takes note of the great significance of the Soviet Union having the hydrogen bomb, and considers what can be done when an arms race and the threat of force are futile. She comes to the conclusion that more and more aid, arms, and control effort must be channeled through the United Nations, and in such a way that each country would have to give up some of its sovereignty. The mere contemplation of the latter requirement is what lends so much agony to the reappraisal. In a sense, Miss Ward is suggesting a course of action for the dilemma posed by Mr. Sulzberger. What is at stake here?

In this work we have been dealing with control in general and control within a kind of unit we have called a polity. All men, it has been argued, are oriented to some polity. We must now turn to the problem of deliberate control of the more remote environment when the object of that control is regarded as external to the polity to which a prospective controller is attached.[2] In order to deal with the dimly perceived more remote environment, man perceives that environment in units. Within the unit, which he both perceives and affects, one kind of control scheme develops and is supported so that the environment may be controlled. And although he also sees the environment beyond in units, his feelings toward these other units are different. He may have varying degrees of indifference toward them, but in any polity some people always see the need to control certain aspects of these other units, and under some conditions all people feel the need to control persons and events in other polities.

It seems quite clear that man's drive to have a tolerably controlled more remote environment knows no bounds, and that the beginning of control effort is to create units. But controlling within a unit that reflects the highest commonly shared allegiance is quite different from controlling people, units, and environments beyond the object of special attachment. The best perspective from which to examine the nature of this control is that of a person attached to one unit who views the rest of the world from the perspective of that attachment. How does an individual extend control to that portion of his environment beyond his strong attachment? In short, how does an individual oriented to one polity control an individual oriented to another?

Only in a limited and metaphorical sense can one polity deal with another polity. In the final analysis, nations dealing with nations must be reduced to individuals dealing with individuals.

Every individual who tries to exercise control and who supports control efforts across national boundaries first perceives the persons with whom he is dealing as members and representatives of another polity. Likewise, his consciousness of his own attachment, his own representative capacity, is sharpened and intensified. Other differences, such as language, race, religion, may also modify the interaction pattern, but consciousness of polity is a distinctive modifier, and probably the most general one. If an individual is antagonistic toward an outside polity he is likely to be antagonistic toward any representative of it. Thus, this outside person is conditioned to react differently from the way he would if these separate polity attachments did not exist. When these differences are intensified by the cultivation of symbolism and formality, cooperative action across boundaries becomes nearly impossible, except in those few instances where the more obvious self-regarding interests of each individual and each polity are reciprocally served. And even then, pure "business deals," as they might be called, are hard to work out. The drive to control persists, but it is expressed in the building of tightly controlled and highly formalized interaction patterns. The first step in this process is to concentrate in the hands of formal spokesmen special instruments for carrying on such relations. And self-regarding acts that do not take account of the polity interest are rigidly forbidden. All international relations are politicized, or governmentalized.

The Constitution of the United States restricts the states in dealing individually with foreign countries. It prohibits a government official from accepting any title or decoration from a foreign country without the approval of Congress, and, although it restricts the definition of treason, it does recognize treason and places no limit on the penalty that can be inflicted. In practice, foreign travel is regulated and foreign trade restricted by the government. Not only do the Constitution and the statutory law impinge upon both official and nonofficial cross-boundary dealings, but traditions and customs of inter-polity relations are quite different from those of intrapolity relations. The stringent regulation of these matters in the United States is not unlike that of other countries. The peculiarities of cross-boundary control are universally recognized and institutionalized.

The formalization and politicization of most of the inter-personal relations that are carried on across national boundaries have a number of consequences. In the first place, persons are formally designated for cross-boundary relations and are given special status, so that they may speak in the name of their country. They can use the other person's perception of it to increase their effectiveness with him, and they may also use this perception to obligate key members of their own polity to support commitments. But where there is strong suspicion of permitting anyone to obligate the members of a polity, the authorized agent is rigidly limited by regulations and traditions as to what he can do and promise with effectiveness. Of course, the effectiveness of a country's agent in controlling the spokesman of another country is directly related to his capacity to speak for and to bind people in his own country. Thus, a spokesman cannot effectively threaten war when his counterpart in another polity knows that he cannot speak for his country on this matter.[3]

Another consequence of dealing across national boundaries has to do with the manner in which the agents are selected.

Since they are chosen deliberately for the function they perform, it is standard practice to emphasize certain qualities in these persons. They must be especially loyal and dedicated to the country they represent. Thus, by the choosing process itself the agents are likely to be persons who attach great importance to differences in allegiance. But because their function is to exercise control over behavior oriented strongly to another polity, they must be thoroughly conversant with the other country. They must know the language and understand the culture, and many of them must live in the other country. As a result of becoming saturated with knowledge and understanding of the other country there is always the likelihood of developing an attachment. Moreover, by living in another country they develop personal ties that transcend national boundaries. Indeed, a part of their effectiveness depends upon acquiring a sympathetic understanding of the other country. This tends to offset their exaggerated nationalism and to keep them under a tension created by the demands of their own polity and those of the one which they are trying to control.

The objects of control and the methods of control are essentially the same across boundaries as they are within boundaries. The object of control is to reduce randomness, to avoid necessity, and to achieve positive purposes. Historically the dominant purpose for exercising this control was to prevent assaults upon the borders of the polity and to prevent acts that would threaten the integrity of the unit. The main concern in all international dealings has always been to prevent war, or to win a war if one does start. Beyond this the kinds of control sought and the kinds of purposes undertaken are infinite.

Interpolity relations are distinguished by the conditions under which control is sought. In interpolity relations the individuals dealing with each other have different polity loyalties. Moreover, each tends to have a special obligation to serve the interest of his polity, and not his own interest if the two are in conflict. This is further complicated by the factor of remoteness. The consequences of an act for the interest of an individual are knowable and predictable and hence there is less difference of opinion involved. But the consequences of acts performed for the sake of a polity are never very clear or predictable, and therefore there are great differences of opinion about these acts. Furthermore, because control is a reciprocal relation there is no control unless the control act elicits a control response. Within a polity an individual may make a concession by giving up something he values for the benefit of the common good, the attachment to polity thus acting as an ameliorating force. In cross-boundary dealings, attachment to polity acts not as an ameliorator but as an exaggerator of differences. The diplomat or foreign negotiator is therefore limited in his control effectiveness to those acts in which advantage is clearly equal. The extraordinary difficulty of exercising cross-boundary control by the method we have called persuasion accounts for the extensive use of proof and coercion in this area of control.

Just as the basic objects of control are not different within and beyond one polity, neither are the control methods different. The deliberate controller still can use the methods of coercion, persuasion, and proof. Let us examine how each of these is used in international affairs.

The drastic method of coercion operates quite differently across boundaries. Instead of force being applied personally and individually, it is applied impersonally and collectively. Its posture is akin to violence and terroristic force, but it tends to be applied systematically and almost wholly for strategic purposes. People are captured and killed in war not for their own acts but because they represent the enemy polity. The main thrust of war is to disorganize the enemy so that he will respond to control even in the face of his attachments. War tends to sanction acts that are usually regarded as immoral, and it tends to regard as immoral acts that are generally regarded as moral. It tends more than anything else to reduce the number of approved self-seeking acts. Fighting a war requires a kind of control and coordination of effort that intensifies those forces which impel an individual to do things without understanding exactly why he does them. Authority has to replace individual conviction and individual merit as a basis for compliance. When war breaks out, most efforts at cooperative interpolity behavior cease and are replaced by systematic efforts to frustrate cooperation. The application of force across boundaries is a highly specialized matter, generally quite different from the use of force within boundaries.

Let us now take a look at persuasion. In our earlier discussion of persuasion we saw that one of the main ways it was used was to cultivate a feeling for a perceived entity and then appeal to people to act on the basis of their affection or hate for the entity. But in the international field this kind of manipulation is used on the agent of a polity. An agent may be led to do something against his own understanding or in the face of his personal values in the name of the country he represents. But even though diplomacy is often portrayed as a process of devious and manipulative acts, the truth is that manipulation probably plays an especially small role in controlling persons across those boundaries. The all-important shared predisposition to automatic obedience and compliance is almost entirely absent. If one agent appeals to another in the name of his love for his country he is suspect and in any event is called upon to prove his case in an established manner. All in all, one can say that it is precisely because a kind of manipulation is so important to control within boundaries that it is so ineffective across boundaries. Thus in interpolity relations the drive to control tends to be expressed in the methods of coercion and proof.

The essence of proof, as we saw earlier, is to get someone to agree to a suggestion by adopting it as his own course of action. Proof is the method *par excellence* of diplomacy. Most of the maneuvering that is associated with diplomacy is really designed to gain access and to gain the best possible conditions under which to make proof efforts effective. Outside of threats of war, and of certain less drastic deprivations, about the only deprivation one diplomat can inflict upon another is to make him feel uncomfortable with a position he holds concerning benefits to his own polity. And even here the proof must make itself effective in the face of the deep attachment to country that the other agent is known to have. Generally speaking, the conditions for effective proof are about as bad as could be deliberately concocted. Predispositions are usually strong and wrong from the perspective of the controller.

All of this suggests what is ostensibly true, that deliberate control of the portion of the more remote environment that lies beyond the boundaries of one's own attachment is extraordinarily difficult and that there is relatively little of it. Spontaneous interaction is nearly impossible, and the posture of individuals toward this environment tends to be adjustive rather than positive. The urge to control becomes especially strong when the dangers inherent in noncontrol become increasingly clear. This is what produces alliances; this is what produced NATO and the United Nations.

What can happen when there is a felt need to extend deliberate control beyond the limits of a single bounded society? Barbara Ward has said in effect that we must loosen or weaken our effective ties to our polities and adopt similar ties to a more comprehensive unit.

When two persons with the same overriding loyalty interact with each other—as when two members of the same polity interact—the common loyalty acts as a mediator, as the setter of limits to the operation of *feelings* and *preferences*. It acts as a predisposer in viewing evidence and providing a perspective for reason; that is to say, logical deductions from evidence. But essentially the common loyalty affects the feelings. It mediates the feeling component in action. Logical, scientific proof per se needs no mediator except the shared conventions of proof. This shared loyalty to an identical entity reduces the self-regarding character of each relevant act of each interactor toward the other. It facilitates cooperation.

When two persons with different objects of loyalty—two members of different polities—interact, every doubt and every predisposition tends to be resolved in a manner that is good for each person's own polity. As we have seen, if the person contemplating an act is a formal agent of his polity, as he usually will be, he will have a special obligation to ask if the act is favorable to his polity. This means that the polity-regarding components will be very high, in terms of his personal preference and feelings, in terms of his image of what is good for his polity, and in terms of what he thinks is expected of him by his principals. Thus, interaction tends to be limited to those situations in which each interactor believes he can get a doubly advantageous deal for his polity. This all tends to emphasize the economic aspect of international acts—no profit, no deal. It further means that the polity-regarding component of acts across boundaries is virtually unlimited. International agencies that do not inculcate a new and more general loyalty have only the effect of permitting all parties to develop a clearer, and in some cases longer-range, notion of what is good for themselves and their polity. This may improve knowledge of consequences, but it does not help resolve differences where knowledge is uncertain or nonexistent. It affords some mediation, but more often it only has the effect of bringing into existence another outside agency which can be opposed to one's own polity.

There is every reason to believe that perceiving and affect-

ing organizational units or entities is a fundamental component in deliberate control, and that this perceiving and affecting is especially important in the deliberate control of the
more remote environment. This raises a question of whether
it is possible to maintain a tolerably stable and deliberately
controllable environment without creating and affecting entities which encompass the spatial and functional distance
over which control is sought.

All human acts have unintended as well as intended consequences. The unintended consequence of acts tends to produce environmental changes, and controlling the unintended
change in the environment in turn requires intended acts.
There is thus a continuous adjustment and modification. One
of the intended consequences of the invention of the atomic
bomb was to protect the integrity of the United States. But
one of the unintended consequences was to hang a threat of
extinction over the human race. It was impossible to have only
the advantages and none of the disadvantages. A tolerably
safe, stable, and friendly more remote environment is not now
possible without the direction and control of all persons who
have custody of the great destructive power of nuclear weapons.

As one contemplates the control problem suggested here
the question comes to mind of whether control of the kind
generally desired is possible without there coming into existence and perception a new and more adequate unit for organizing the more remote environment. Must there now be a
new and more comprehensive object of dominant loyalty? Or
is there reason to believe that we have reached a point in deliberate control of others, and of ourselves, where a commonly
affected entity is no longer necessary, where that which needs
to be controlled will be selectively and effectively controlled
directly by common consent? If past experience is to be a
guide, proof and dominant force must be supplemented by

that kind of manipulation of feelings which revolves around loyalty and allegiance to an appropriate unit of the more remote environment. There must be a mediation of self-regarding acts which affects all whose control is felt to be necessary to provide the tolerably safe, stable, and friendly environment. This seems to call for a new and more general entity which not only comes into existence as a resulting pattern of actual interaction, but which at the same time comes into existence as a shaper of individual minds. Experience gives no comfort to those who hope that adequate control can be affected without the new loyalty, with all that implies for the moderating of the old loyalty. When the historic process of creating new and different entities of overriding loyalty is contemplated it is hard to be too optimistic about the intermediate-range future.

What would be the signs of the rise of a new loyalty-commanding unit, the rise of a new polity? It should be recalled that every social formation has both a resultant aspect and an instrumental aspect. Much of the increased interaction between agents and members of societies in recent years is unquestionably forging new interaction patterns that tend to form units and to have at least functional boundaries. The United Nations, NATO, and the various other regional and specialized pacts are all examples of an extraordinary activity pattern development across polity boundaries. But there is little sign that much is happening in the perceiving and affecting realm. If anything, events of recent years have served to sharpen perceptions of polities as they now exist. The Wilsonian emphasis upon self-determination gave a great lift to narrower rather than broader perceived units. The name United Nations Organization was quickly changed to the United Nations, presumably because it was thought to be a more attractive title for an entity which it was hoped would evoke some loyalty. The Korean war, as a United Nations war, was largely an accident but it served to increase the loyalty-evoking power of the United Nations. The role of the UN in the creation of Israel and the mediating of the subsequent disputes may also be important. The recent action in the Congo is still another example of the kind of development that might suggest a new object of loyalty.

The new dimension of the remote environment in our own time is undoubtedly created by the threat of nuclear weapons. A remote environmental factor is now capable of suddenly disorganizing the life of the individual. Thus there is a growing concern with the events at the periphery of the globe, and with events that can be deliberately brought about by the exercise of human will. Local police forces and national armies can no longer reduce randomness in the more remote environment. Specifically we are now faced with an urgent need to control the behavior of the Communist world. And this world is faced with a need to control us. Is the mutual control that is needed, and on the scale needed, possible without the development of a common loyalty to a common entity, a loyalty that will mediate feelings and preferences, a loyalty that will prevent *individuals* from doing what they would like to do, or cause them to do what they would not otherwise think of doing?

It will be clear that a new loyalty-evoking entity has emerged when men begin to argue that the good of a new entity requires people to behave in certain ways. Present talk about the destruction of the world may indicate that the entity of dominant concern is the world itself. A higher loyalty to "the world" is implied, if only by emphasis on its nondestruction. Of course, this is purely negative, but probably all extensions of control over the more remote environment have initially been negative in the same sense. Randomness in the more remote environment must first be reduced before more positive and diverse purposes can be achieved.

In view of what has been said it is not hard to see why Barbara Ward should call for more cooperation through the instrumentality of the United Nations. Whatever the fate of the United Nations, it seems clear that some entity such as "world" will have to come into existence in the *feelings* of individuals throughout the world if deliberate control is to offset the possibility of deliberate or accidental destruction. The psychological agonies that such a process will produce are painful to contemplate.

In view of what has been said, it is not hard to envisage...

Notes

PART ONE

Chapter 1

1. *Behavioral Science*, Vol. II (1957), pp. 201–15.
2. The basic distinction suggested here is related to that developed by C. H. Cooley in *Social Organization* (New York: Scribners, 1909). It is also related to the distinction made by Ferdinand Tönnies between *Gemeinschaft* and *Gesellschaft* in *Community and Association* (London: Routledge and Kegan Paul, 1955). The use of "more remote environment" in this context was presented in less-developed form in my *The Study of Political Parties* (New York: Random House, 1955), especially in Chapter 6. A remarkably similar approach was simultaneously but coincidentally developed by Peter Laslett in "The Face to Face Society" in P. Laslett, ed., *Philosophy, Politics, and Society* (New York: Macmillan, 1956), pp. 157–84.
3. New York: Henry Holt, 1926.
4. Much needs to be done to isolate the "intended" act and to ascertain differences in such acts and in the consequences of the acts. Dorwin Cartwright states: "It is evident that O may produce an act which sets up forces in P's life space even though O had no intention of influencing P. The distinction between intentional and unintentional influence played an important part in the research of Lippitt, Polan-

sky, Redl, and Rosen . . . who distinguished between 'behavioral contagion,' as the spontaneous pickup or imitation of behavior initiated by one child when he displayed no intention of getting the others to do what he did, and 'direct influence,' as behavior which had the manifest objective of affecting the behavior of another. Observers were able to code there two kinds of acts at acceptable levels of reliability, and significant empirical differences were found between the two kinds of acts. It would seem that the intentionality of acts is of critical importance in processes of influence and power" (Dorwin Cartwright, ed., *Studies in Social Power* [Ann Arbor: Research Center for Group Dynamics, Institute for Social Research, Univ. of Michigan, 1959], pp. 200–1). The research cited in this passage is reported in *Human Relations*, Vol. V (1952), pp. 37–64. It, of course, deals with control of effect by intended acts in a face-to-face situation, and in view of the differences between proximity and remoteness that are hypothesized it might not apply; but it is at least suggestive. The notion of intentionality is also implied in the distinction made by Robert K. Merton between latent and manifest function and dysfunction, in *Social Theory and Social Structure*, Rev. Ed. (Glencoe, Ill.: The Free Press, 1957), pp. 60–84.

5. *Atlantic Monthly* (December, 1952), pp. 25–30.

6. *Politics, Economics and Welfare* (New York: Harper, 1953).

Chapter 2

1. *Human Nature and Conduct* (New York: Henry Holt, 1922), p. 278.

2. Boston: Houghton Mifflin, 1957.

3. *Ibid.*, p. ix.

4. *Ibid.*, p. 24.

5. *Dominations and Powers* (New York: Scribners, 1951), pp. viii–ix.

Chapter 3

1. For a recent and provocative discussion of structure in general, but particularly as it is related to perception, see Floyd Allport, *Theories of Perception and the Concept of Structure* (New York: Wiley, 1955), especially Chapter 21.

2. There is a vast literature on this development. See especially, Frederich Meinecke, *Die Idee der Staatsräson in der Neueren Geschichte* (2nd German ed., 1925), translated by Douglass Scott as *Machiavellism, the Doctrine of Raison d'état and Its Place in Modern History* (New Haven: Yale University Press, 1957).

3. *Of the Laws of Ecclesiastical Polity* (New York: Dutton, 1922).

4. *The Vocabulary of Politics* (London: Penguin Books, 1953), p. 46.

5. See Floyd Allport, *Theories of Perception*, Chapter 21.

6. *Ibid.*, Chapter 2.

7. For a useful attempt to specify the objective aspects of polity, see K. W. Deutsch, *Nationalism and Social Communication* (New York: Wiley, 1953).

8. Talcott Parsons, "Pattern Variables Revisited: A Response to Robert Dubin," in *American Sociological Review*, Vol. 25 (August, 1960), pp. 467–83.

9. Allport, *Theories of Perception*, p. 41.

10. *Ibid.*, p. 43.

11. Kenneth E. Boulding, *The Image* (Ann Arbor: The University of Michigan Press, 1956), p. 3.

12. *Ibid.*, pp. 5–6.

13. Allport, *Theories of Perception*, p. 64.

14. *Ibid.*, p. 65.

15. Boulding, *The Image*, p. 111.

16. See the provocative discussion of this topic in Ernst Cassirer, *The Myth of the State* (New Haven: Yale University Press), especially Chapter 4.

17. Dennis v. United States, 341 U.S. 494, 1950.

PART TWO

1. *Political Science Quarterly*, Vol. LXV (June, 1950), No. 2.

2. Quoted in Lyman Bryson, Louis Finkelstein, and R. M. MacIver, eds., *Symbols and Society* (New York: Harper, 1955), pp. 112–13.

PART THREE
Chapter 8

1. Chester Barnard uses the phrase "executive function" in *The Functions of the Executive* (Cambridge, Mass.: Harvard University Press, 1938).

2. New York: McGraw-Hill, 1952.

PART FOUR
Chapter 10

1. Francis Coker, *Recent Political Thought* (New York: Appleton-Century, 1934), p. 381.

2. *Escape from Freedom* (New York: Farrar and Rinehart, 1941), p. 232.

Chapter 11

1. London: Oxford University Press, 1947.
2. *The Governmental Process* (New York: Knopf, 1951), pp. 33–43.
3. See Truman, *The Governmental Process,* and Earl Latham, *The Group Basis of Politics* (Ithaca, N.Y.: Cornell University Press, 1952).
4. New York: Harper, 1956.

Chapter 12

1. *The Person and the Common Good* (New York: Scribners, 1947), p. 5.
2. *Moral Man and Immoral Society* (New York: Scribners, 1932), p. 81.
3. *Saturday Review of Literature,* July 28, 1951, p. 6.
4. Chicago: University of Chicago Press, 1944, p. 56.
5. Volume XIII, p. 235.

Chapter 14

1. *New York Times Magazine,* July 22, 1956.
2. J. N. Rosenau, my colleague at Douglass College, has made interesting use of the concept of calculated control in international relations. See his *Calculated Control as a Unifying Concept in the Study of International Politics and Foreign Policy* (Princeton: Center for International Politics, Princeton University, 1963).
3. For an excellent discussion of strategy, especially in the international arena, see Thomas Schelling, *The Strategy of Conflict* (Cambridge, Mass.: Harvard University Press, 1960), especially Chapter I. Schelling argues most convincingly that the premise of what he calls rational behavior is especially useful for the production of theory. In his general treatment, however, Schelling does not seem to take adequate account of the polity attachment or the remoteness component, as they are defined here.

Index